CREATIVE INVESTIGATIONS
IN EARLY MATH

Angela Eckhoff, PhD

D1159550

Gryphon House
www.gryphonhouse.com

Published by Gryphon House Inc.
P. O. Box 10, Lewisville, NC 27023
800.638.0928; fax 877.638.7576
www.gryphonhouse.com

Bulk Purchase

Gryphon House books are available for special premiums and sales promotions as well as for fund-raising use. Special editions or book excerpts also can be created to specifications. For details, call 800.638.0928.

Disclaimer

Gryphon House Inc. cannot be held responsible for damage, mishap, or injury incurred during the use of or because of activities in this book. Appropriate and reasonable caution and adult supervision of children involved in activities and corresponding to the age and capability of each child involved are recommended at all times. Do not leave children unattended at any time. Observe safety and caution at all times.

Library of Congress Cataloging-in-Publication Data
Names: Eckhoff, Angela, 1974-
Title: Creative investigations in early math / Angela Eckhoff, PhD.
Description: Lewisville, NC : Gryphon House, [2017] | Includes index.
Identifiers: LCCN 2016046013 | ISBN 9780876597293
Subjects: LCSH: Mathematics--Study and teaching (Early childhood) |
    Mathematical recreations. | Creative thinking in children.
Classification: LCC QA135.6 .E3275 2017 | DDC 372.7--dc23 LC record available at
https://lccn.loc.gov/2016046013

Contents

Acknowledgments. iv

Introduction. 1

1. Developing a Creative Math Environment 13

2. Numbers and Number Sense. 19

3. Computation 36

4. Geometry and Spatial Sense 51

5. Measurement 76

6. Data Collection and Statistics 92

7. Patterns and Relationships 105

Index 117

Acknowledgments

I would like to express my gratitude for all of the teachers and children who have shared their classrooms with me as I have worked to better understand the role of creativity during the early childhood years. Thank you for your continued inspiration and for sharing your excitement and enthusiasm for learning.

Introduction

"Look at me!" shouts Clay to his friends Shawn and Cassidy. The two children are standing down below as Clay climbs a small set of stairs leading to a higher platform at the Nashville Zoo's Jungle Gym feature. The Jungle Gym includes a 35-foot-tall wooden Tree of Life climbing structure designed to encourage children to explore different zoo animals' methods of locomotion. "You climb like a monkey!" observes Clay's teacher, Kathleen, who is standing nearby. "C'mon, climb like monkeys," encourages Clay to his two friends waiting at the bottom of the climbing structure. The children quickly climb up to the platform where Clay is waiting. Together, the trio decides to climb to the rope netting to swing like monkeys. As the children navigate their way across the rope netting with monkey-inspired movements, Kathleen narrates their actions using position words: "Awesome, Clay! You are nearing the top." "Shawn is beside Cassidy now." "Keep going to the right. You've got it!"

From his vantage point on the rope netting, Shawn spots a large, open-mouthed snake structure on the other side of the Jungle Gym. After Shawn points out his discovery to his friends, he encourages the others to join him inside the snake. The three begin to make their way off the rope netting to the wooden platform. Watching the trio from the ground, Kathleen encourages Shawn to think about the movement of a snake. "You're going to have to change from a monkey to a snake. What was the word the zookeeper taught us about how snakes move?" She prompts, "It starts with an s." "Slither! Slowly slither," recalls Shawn. Kathleen moves with the group over to the snake and encourages them to enact slithering movements as she uses more position words. "Slither through there. Cassidy is slithering on top of the snake! Yikes, these snakes keep slithering down to the ground!"

As the experiences of Clay, Shawn, and Cassidy demonstrate, everyday activities can provide playful opportunities for teachers to introduce and reinforce math skills. In this example, Kathleen was able to narrate the children's natural movements using descriptive position words that are central to understanding spatial relationships. She supported the children's creative play and worked to encourage them to apply what they knew about

Children find interesting ways to climb up the Nashville Zoo's Jungle Gym.

The snake head at the Nashville Zoo inspires children to move around in a slithering motion.

animal locomotion while providing the language of geometry to extend and support their understandings.

Preschoolers can learn math concepts naturally as they become intrigued with learning about their world and how it works. As an educator, you can fuel young children's desire for knowledge and intentionally encourage creative explorations that help preschoolers build math skills every day in the different environments they encounter. This book is designed to provide you with knowledge and lesson ideas that support young children's development of mathematics understanding via inquiry and creative-thinking skills. Creative-thinking skills can be found in all aspects of young children's playful engagement and include imagining, exploration, visualization, design, divergent thinking, and solution finding. Teaching mathematics in a linear, fact-based fashion is not ideal for children ages three to five. Instead, they will thrive in classrooms that promote hands-on experimentation and intentionally encourage minds-on learning experiences. Young children build early mathematics understandings through guided and independent investigations that encourage them to be actively involved in meaningful ways. These investigations can be large and sustained over a period of time—such as creating maps of the classroom or school—or they can be part of a planned lesson activity—such as helping measure ingredients to make playdough. The most important aspect of these investigations is that the children are engaged both physically and mentally—hands-on and minds-on engagement. This book highlights the role of the early childhood educator as guide and facilitator in the planning, implementation, and assessment of creative mathematics experiences. *Creative Investigations in Early Math* will support your development of these types of classroom experiences in the following ways:

- You can link mathematics content and inquiry-based learning.

- You can plan cooperative math lessons that will engage all children in your classroom.

- You can find ways to support children's math learning in everyday classroom experiences.

- You can recognize children's mathematical thinking in order to build on their current levels of understanding.

- You can document children's knowledge development with a variety of classroom work samples.

Assessment is an important element in mathematics teaching and learning, as you can gain insight into what works with particular children and what new strategies you can try as you strive to promote more-advanced understanding. Conversations, children's drawings, and other types of classroom work are all representative forms of children's thinking and understanding. By exploring children's work to better understand their thinking, you can create experiences that build upon and deepen children's mathematical understanding.

Playful Learning

Play is an important element for learning in early childhood because it helps young children learn about themselves, their environment, people they interact with, and the world around them. Playful learning encourages children to explore and experiment in situations in which they feel comfortable taking risks and delving into the unknown. When children explore, experiment, and cooperate through play, they learn about how the world works. Children need teachers who are supportive of children's play and who work to carefully identify play situations where teacher guidance or involvement will be welcome and positive.

Young children make use of the information gathered during their everyday experiences by bringing these ideas into their play to further experiment and clarify their understanding. This process is child driven, and your role is to support preschoolers' curiosity. Using intentional pedagogical practices, you can create early childhood classrooms that honor the ways in which children learn, explore, and play. As you carefully observe children's play and recognize their current stages of understanding, you can scaffold their thinking by questioning, supplying materials that encourage experimentation, and providing opportunities for guided learning.

Early Mathematics Experiences

Young children love to actively explore as they seek to understand what is going on around them. As they investigate their environment, they can build mathematical knowledge during everyday interactions. For example, when preschoolers place one plate in front of each child at lunch, sing counting songs, or play board games with friends, they are building their content knowledge as well as their mathematical identities. The concept of *positive mathematics identities* is important because young children's early experiences with mathematics can influence their confidence in their ability to understand and use mathematics in later school years.

Early mathematics learning can challenge children to explore ideas about patterns and relationships, order and predictability, and measurement. Supportive instruction occurs in classroom environments that are conversationally rich, encourage children's thinking, and respect and nurture children's explorations. It is important to keep in mind that mathematics appears in all aspects of children's play experiences so that the support you provide children will reinforce and extend children's understandings in an authentic way.

The International Academy of Education (IAE) emphasizes ten principles of effective mathematics teaching that you can apply to your preschool classrooms. The IAE principles are listed in column 1 of the following table; you will also find associated action steps preschool teachers can take to support children's mathematics learning experiences.

Principles and Action Steps for Effective Preschool Math Teaching

Teaching Principles	Action Steps for Preschool Classrooms
Caring classroom communities that are focused on mathematical goals help develop students' mathematical identities and proficiencies.	• Build a community of trust where young children feel safe asking questions and exploring ideas. • Build classroom math experiences around clearly defined goals and aims.
Effective teachers provide students with opportunities to work both independently and collaboratively to make sense of ideas.	• Provide a balance of mathematical learning experiences for the individual student, small groups, and the whole class.
Effective teachers plan mathematics learning experiences that enable students to build on their existing proficiencies, interests, and experiences.	• Connect classroom mathematics experiences to children's existing understandings and knowledge. • Use children's misconceptions and errors as building blocks for developing deeper understandings.
Effective teachers understand that the tasks and examples they select influence how students come to view, develop, use, and make sense of mathematics	• Provide mathematics experiences that encourage original thinking and encourage children to struggle with ideas. • Focus on thinking versus providing the right answer. • Provide children many opportunities to practice what they are learning throughout the day.
Effective teachers support students in creating connections between different ways of solving problems, between mathematical representations and topics, and between mathematics and everyday experiences.	• Provide opportunities for children to use mathematics knowledge in their everyday experiences. • Emphasize the links between different mathematical ideas and learning experiences.

(continues next page)

(continued from previous page)

Teaching Principles	Action Steps for Preschool Classrooms
Effective teachers use a range of assessment practices to make students' thinking visible and to support students' learning.	• Provide opportunities for children to document their own thinking during learning experiences. • Pay close attention to children's progress and take notes to document their thinking. • Take the time to listen to children's responses, ask questions, and provide supportive feedback to all children.
Effective teachers are able to facilitate classroom dialogue that is focused on mathematical argumentation.	• Encourage children to explain their thinking verbally or through drawing and writing.
Effective teachers shape mathematical language by modeling appropriate terms and communicating their meaning in ways students understand.	• Model mathematics language in the classroom.
Effective teachers carefully select tools and representations to provide support for students' thinking.	• Provide children with an appropriate variety of mathematics learning materials.
Effective teachers develop and use sound knowledge as a basis for initiating learning and responding to the mathematical needs of all of their students.	• Build your own understanding of mathematics content and curricular goals to make informed decisions. • Seek out professional development opportunities to build your understandings of content and pedagogy.

Source for column 1: Anthony, Glenda, and Margaret Walshaw. 2009. *Effective Pedagogy in Mathematics.* Educational Practices Series–19. Belgium: International Academy of Education. http://www.ibe.unesco.org/fileadmin/user_upload/Publications/Educational_Practices/EdPractices_19.pdf

Creative Investigations in Early Math

Guided Inquiry

Inquiry-based learning can play a central role in the development of meaningful learning opportunities as children explore emerging skills in early mathematics. Contrary to traditional notions of the teacher's role as a teller of information, teachers in inquiry classrooms perform the roles of guide, facilitator, and provocateur by asking questions and designing meaningful lessons built on student interests. A teacher's ability to listen to her students builds the foundation for guided inquiry in the classroom.

When using an inquiry-driven approach to mathematics learning, a teacher works closely with children to support observation and listening skills, encourage individual expression, and promote problem exploration. This approach requires planning and intensive teaching on the part of the teacher as well as attentiveness and active engagement on the part of the children. As teachers work to pose questions to prompt interest, children will work to delve further into their understandings through cycles of questioning, exploration, and documentation. In inquiry-driven classrooms, teacher questioning patterns associated with traditional models of teaching are set aside in favor of open-ended, exploratory questioning. Instead of asking who can tell what the shape is named, you might ask

the children to describe the shape to you or ask them how they know it is a certain shape. You then could promote deeper thinking by asking the children what they would like to know about the shape. As you move away from the "guess what's in my head" questioning patterns, you can model for the children a higher level of questioning that encourages them to think about what they know and don't know, when they need to find more information, and whether new information supports or extends their previous understandings.

The concept of *possibility thinking* encourages teachers to consider how questions, play, supportive classrooms, imagination, innovation, risk taking, and self-determination—core elements identified by researchers Teresa Cremin, Pamela Burnard, and Anna Craft—affect the processes of thinking and learning. Possibility thinking involves a dynamic interplay between children and teachers in the following ways:

- **Questioning**—Teachers acknowledge and celebrate children's questions. Teachers pose questions that encourage inquiry.

- **Play**—Children have opportunities for extended play periods.

- **Immersion**—Children are immersed in a benign environment free from criticism and mockery.

- **Innovation**—Teachers closely observe innovations in children's thinking in order to prompt and encourage.

- **Imagination**—Children have ample opportunities to meld imagination and classroom learning.

- **Self-determination and risk taking**—Teachers encourage deep involvement and risk taking, and the children support these behaviors.

The lessons you encounter in this book encourage you to carefully consider your interactions with young children as well as the classroom environment you create together. The interplay among children, teachers, and the classroom environment are all central to the process of learning. The following table suggests action steps that can help you in creating positive and creative math learning experiences for preschoolers.

Promoting Guided Inquiry and Creative Math Learning

Classroom Components	Teacher Actions
Physical environment	• Thoughtfully include a variety of manipulatives, blocks, natural materials, and digital media for free exploration.
Role of the teacher	• Develop a supportive environment for playful learning, experimentation, and risk taking. • Closely observe children's play and exploration, using formative assessments. • Ask thoughtful questions and provide provocations to expand and clarify children's thinking.
Relationships among peers	• Provide opportunities for collaborative experiences. • Demonstrate respect for children's work. • Promote opportunities for play and exploration.
Structure of mathematics lessons and experiences	• Provide opportunities for individual and group experiences. • Maintain flexible scheduling for lesson lengths based on children's responses and interests. • Provide for repeated mathematics experiences. • Promote opportunities for children to make their thinking visible (using concrete manipulatives, math journals, digital photography, and so on). • Extend familiar lessons and concepts to build proficiency and flexibility of student understanding.

Organization of the Book

Setting up the classroom environment to encourage math explorations is important. Chapter 1 provides guidance on organizing the math center and the classroom. Each of the following chapters is based on a particular mathematics content area: numbers and number sense, computation, geometry and spatial sense, measurement, data collection and statistics, and patterns and relationships. In each chapter, you will see a listing of the National Council of Teachers of Mathematics (NCTM) content learning standards. In addition to the particular content information, NCTM recommends that teachers provide opportunities for children to meet process standards in the areas of problem solving, reasoning and proof, communication, connections, and representation. These process standards align with the inquiry-driven, creative mathematics experiences recommended throughout this book. Alongside the NCTM process standards and expectations, you will see more-specific approaches for supporting preschool math learning in those areas.

Supporting NCTM Process Standards

NCTM Process Standard	Expectations for Students	Supportive Approaches in the Early Childhood Classroom
Problem solving	• Build new mathematical knowledge through problem solving. • Solve problems that arise in mathematics and in other contexts. • Apply and adapt a variety of appropriate strategies to solve problems. • Monitor and reflect on the process of mathematical problem solving.	Provide opportunities for children to ask questions, work out planning and trials, work in pairs and small groups, and plan experiments.

NCTM Process Standard	Expectations for Students	Supportive Approaches in the Early Childhood Classroom
Reasoning and proof	• Recognize reasoning and proof as fundamental aspects of mathematics. • Make and investigate mathematical conjectures. • Develop and evaluate mathematical arguments and proofs. • Select and use various types of reasoning and methods of proof.	Provide opportunities for children to document their thinking through drawing and writing and to share their thoughts with large and small groups.
Communication	• Organize and consolidate their mathematical thinking through communication. • Communicate their mathematical thinking coherently and clearly to peers, teachers, and others. • Analyze and evaluate the mathematical thinking and strategies of others. • Use the language of mathematics to express mathematical ideas precisely.	Provide opportunities for children to share their problem-solving experiences, and encourage and support children's use of mathematics language.
Connections	• Recognize and use connections among mathematical ideas. • Understand how mathematical ideas interconnect and build on one another to produce a coherent whole. • Recognize and apply mathematics in contexts outside of mathematics.	Provide opportunities for children to use math in everyday experiences and in other content areas. Revisit math lessons mulitiple times to encourage mastery and promote confidence.

(continues next page)

(continued from previous page)

NCTM Process Standard	Expectations for Students	Supportive Approaches in the Early Childhood Classroom
Representation	• Create and use representations to organize, record, and communicate mathematical ideas. • Select, apply, and translate among mathematical representations to solve problems. • Use representations to model and interpret physical, social, and mathematical phenomena.	Provide opportunities for children to represent their thinking through drawing, writing, and verbal experiences.

Source: National Council of Teachers of Mathematics. 2000. *Principles and Standards for School Mathematics.* Reston, VA: NCTM. Adapted with permission.

This book shares practical strategies designed to help you encourage preschoolers' learning of mathematics processes and content. At the beginning of chapters 2 through 7, you will find information that will familiarize you with the particular chapter topic. You will also find classroom vignettes to help bring the content and teaching strategies to life. Woven into each of those chapters are preschool math lessons based on best practices for guided inquiry and creative thinking. You will also find guidance on content-specific math centers, whole-group experiences, and recommended children's books related to each chapter's content.

1
Developing a Creative Math Environment

Early childhood educators have essential roles in the development of children's creative-thinking skills because they can either create supportive classroom environments or classrooms in which children's creative skills are stifled. Teachers can incorporate creative learning experiences by designing lessons that include opportunities for critical thinking and reflection while also maintaining a focus on student interest. In a classroom environment, creativity should be viewed as a learning process that encourages social interaction, promotes individual ownership of ideas, and requires children to document and report on their thinking and experiences. When young children have opportunities to personally engage with challenging, reflective learning experiences, they can build their critical- and creative-thinking skills.

The lesson ideas and classroom vignettes shared throughout this book incorporate opportunities to help children understand the concepts of *numeracy, classification, comparing, sequencing, shape, structure, location, motion,* and *transformation.* The lessons include critical elements of inquiry and creative thinking—open-ended tasks, activities involving social interaction, and opportunities for children's reflection and elaboration. In other words, the lessons in this book will encourage you to plan and implement math experiences that teach children ways to think rather than narrowly focus on teaching children what to think. Open-ended tasks provide young learners with opportunities to experiment with new ideas and engage in inquiry. Because open-ended tasks promote idea experimentation, they encourage children to focus on the processes of learning rather than the need to arrive at a single correct answer. Gaining experience with idea experimentation can help children accept ambiguity, be willing to make mistakes, and gain confidence in their problem-solving abilities. Likewise, providing opportunities for small-group work and social interaction is a crucial component of creative thinking. Working in pairs or small groups will help to promote brainstorming and allow children to learn from and with each other. Such tasks will also support children's experiences with reflection and idea elaboration. These skills are important cognitive tools that allow preschoolers to learn from their own experiences and examine their own learning process. Employing these components of creativity in the classroom will help to create a rich, engaging learning environment for all of the children.

Designing the Math Learning Center

In addition to planning and implementing targeted mathematics learning experiences in early childhood classrooms, it is important to structure the classroom environment to support children's everyday explorations in numeracy, geometry, estimation, problem solving, and measurement. The math center can be a permanent or moveable area in your classroom where math materials and manipulatives are available for children to freely explore. Although the center does not need to be large, it is important for the materials to be engaging and well-organized to support children's independent explorations. Consider the following elements for your math center:

- **Work space**—Ensure that children have enough space to use materials and manipulatives without becoming frustrated. For example, puzzles can be an effective way for children to experiment with size, directionality, and patterning, but children will need to have room to lay out all of the pieces and explore them for an extended period of time. The size of your mathematics center will also determine whether children will work individually, in pairs, or in small groups.

- **Storage and display of mathematics materials**—If you have enough room, the math center location can also be used to store mathematics materials permanently for children and teachers to easily access. If space is limited, materials can be easily rotated in and out to support the children's current interests and curricular experiences. If you have wall space near the math center, use it to display the charts, graphs, and children's work generated during classroom mathematics lessons. You can encourage children to use these displays to support and extend their explorations.

- **Books and math journals**—Place relevant children's mathematics books in the center in addition to the children's math journals.

An intentional and well-designed mathematics center will provide children opportunities to extend and continually explore the concepts introduced during math lessons at their own pace and interest level. Revisiting ideas and concepts during play is important to the process of knowledge building. Design your center so that children can do the following:

- Explore and learn based on their interests

- Engage in discovery and construction of meaning

- Extend activities from the lessons

- Explore concepts from the lessons or related concepts in depth

- Connect math to daily experiences

Ideas for Managing the Center

You can optimize children's individual and small-group work in the math center in these ways:

- Involve the children in the setup and maintenance of the center. Carefully organize the materials so that the children can help keep them organized after use.

- Carefully consider the number of children that the center can support at a given time.

- Ensure that children have enough work time while in the center. Exploration takes time. Provide them with repeated opportunities to return to the center.

- Share and discuss your expectations that children respect and use materials carefully.

- Ensure that children have opportunities to share and discuss their center-based explorations and discoveries. Math journals are an effective tool for children to document their work.

Materials and Manipulatives for Math Explorations

Consider stocking the following types of items in the center:

- **Numbers and Number Sense**—counters of various sizes and colors; sorting trays; dice; abacuses; number boards; glass cabochons of various sizes, colors, and shapes; and natural materials such as leaves, pinecones, seashells, and rocks of various sizes and colors

- **Computation**—a cash register, realistic coins and paper money, pads of paper and pencils for recording numbers, and counters of various sizes and colors

- **Geometry and Spatial Sense**—puzzles, shape blocks of various sizes and colors, maps, and materials for mapmaking

- **Measurement**—measuring tape, rulers, balances, clocks, calendars, and materials for nonstandard measurement such as string

- **Patterns and Relationships**—sorting sets and counters of various shapes and colors, and other sorting items such as rocks, seashells, mosaic tiles, and buttons

- **Data Collection and Analysis**—various collections of items and containers for sorting

In addition to these materials, digital technologies can be a valuable part of early mathematics learning. These may include tablet and computer-based apps and games, interactive whiteboards, and digital cameras.

Providing access to a variety of materials beyond traditional resources can broaden and extend children's explorations. Consider the theory of *loose parts* proposed by architect Simon Nicholson in the 1970s. Loose parts are materials without a predetermined purpose that can be moved, carried, combined, redesigned, and taken apart and put back together in multiple ways. Loose parts can be used alone or combined with other materials and can be both man-made and natural. In your preschool classroom, loose parts that can be used in geometry and spatial explorations might include blocks, sand, playdough, recycled paper tubes, paper scraps, ribbons, lids, wood scraps, wire, cardboard, large buttons, glass cabochons, string, sticks, large beads, and straws. Take care to include only items that are appropiate for your students and that will not present choking hazards. Including loose parts as part of early geometric explorations promotes independent investigations and allows children opportunities to manipulate objects. Expanding children's access to nontraditional materials can provide a wider range of learning opportunities in the classroom. Many of the examples from early childhood classrooms shared in the following chapters involve a combination of traditional mathematics learning materials, digital technologies, and loose parts.

2
Numbers and Number Sense

Number sense is a core component of early mathematics learning and will form the foundation for children's later math learning. Young children experience the concept of *number* throughout their everyday experiences and routines, whether they are playing board games, passing out materials, or finding their place in line. These daily experiences provide opportunities to count and compare numbers in ways that are personally meaningful. Although everyday experiences with numbers are important, they are not enough to build a deep understanding. In addition, you will want to intentionally design activities that can build children's understandings of number sense and operations. Opportunities for extended investigations will help children develop a robust, flexible understanding of the concept of number.

Understanding the concept of number is a complex process for young children. Preschoolers can learn to recite their numbers—one, two, three, four, five—well before they understand that the number 4 represents four different objects. Similarly, young children learn to sing along to the ABC song before they can recognize the letter C in print. You can support children's developing understanding by creating many opportunities for them to explore numbers with concrete objects. In this way, you can scaffold the process of counting and identifying numerals by name.

As you plan activities involving numbers and number sense, consider the NCTM guiding principals and standards related to number and operations. It is important to note that the NCTM Principles and Standards for School Mathematics that are listed throughout this book refer to standards and expectations for children in prekindergarten through second grade. Pre-K children are not expected to master these concepts. It is appropriate for you to use the standards and expectations to guide the children's introduction to the various mathematics content areas. Early math experiences are important because they lay the foundation for later mathematics learning, but the primary importance of these experiences is that they offer opportunities for understanding math concepts right now. You can work to support engaging, challenging, and enjoyable math experiences that introduce a range of mathematics content by reviewing the standards and thinking about the connections between the lessons you design and the NCTM expectations for student learning.

Number and Operations

Understand numbers, ways of representing numbers, relationships among numbers, and number systems

In pre-K through grade 2 all students should—

- count with understanding and recognize "how many" in sets of objects;

- use multiple models to develop initial understandings of place value and the base-ten number system;

- develop understanding of the relative position and magnitude of whole numbers and of ordinal and cardinal numbers and their connections;

- develop a sense of whole numbers and represent and use them in flexible ways, including relating, composing, and decomposing numbers;

- connect number words and numerals to the quantities they represent, using various physical models and representations;

- understand and represent commonly used fractions, such as $1/4$, $1/3$, and $1/2$.

Creative Investigations in Early Math

Understand meanings of operations and how they relate to one another

In pre-K through grade 2 all students should—

- understand various meanings of addition and subtraction of whole numbers and the relationship between the two operations;

- understand the effects of adding and subtracting whole numbers;

- understand situations that entail multiplication and division, such as equal groupings of objects and sharing equally.

Source: National Council of Teachers of Mathematics. 2000. *Principles and Standards for School Mathematics.* Reston, VA: NCTM. Reproduced with permission.

One-to-One Correspondence and Cardinality

Counting objects involves much more than just reciting a string of number words. Children must be able to pair one number word with each object to be counted. The principle of *one-to-one correspondence* holds that each item must be counted once and only once. Prior to having an understanding of one-to-one correspondence, young children will rely on their visual perception to estimate number. This is known as a *global level of quantification*, which refers to the ability to develop an approximation, or estimate, of quantity. Once children can point to individual objects while counting or line up objects for one-to-one matches, they have moved to the one-to-one correspondence level of quantification. One-to-one correspondence is necessary to develop a sense of *cardinality*, which is the understanding that when counting a group of items the number word applied to the last object represents the total amount of the group. Once children possess an understanding of *cardinality* and can use counting to determine specific amounts of objects in a group, they have reached the *counting level of quantification*.

Vignette for Understanding: Counting Together

In Mrs. Thomas's classroom, Braden and Vanessa are sitting with the teacher at a small table in the dramatic-play area. On the table in front of them is a mix of grocery store items—plastic fruits and vegetables, small dry-goods boxes, and empty drink containers. Braden wants to put the food in groups to clean up, so Mrs. Thomas suggests that the children count each kind of food and then put them into separate baskets to help organize the shelves. The children agree, and together they count the fruits and vegetables first. Each time one of them puts an item in the basket, they call out the associated number word (one, two, three, and so on). At one point, Vanessa is preparing to add an apple to the basket, but she has lost track of the number they are on. Mrs. Thomas pauses and says, "Let's count the ones we already have in here so you know what number that apple is." Using her finger, she touches each piece of fruit in the basket as she counts. Braden joins in while Vanessa waits excitedly for a pause as the last item in the basket is counted. "Six!" she exclaims as she adds the sixth item, the apple, to the basket.

Reflection

As Mrs. Thomas's interactions demonstrate, early childhood teachers can support children's understanding of one-to-one correspondence and cardinality by taking advantage of the many informal opportunities for learning that occur throughout the day. Modeling counting alongside children during play activities is an effective way to give them opportunities to practice and learn alongside their peers.

Quantification

In order to develop their understanding of numbers and the relationships among numbers, young children need opportunities to develop and use quantification skills. Teachers can support the development of quantification—to determine or express the quantity of a group—by creating and presenting opportunities to children throughout the day. By engaging in playful mathematics experiences with peers that involve creating object sets and adding objects to and subtracting objects from the set, children are able to test strategies and learn from other children's strategies. During early childhood, children who engage in quantification experiences develop an important mathematics skill known as *subitizing*, which is the ability to identify how many objects are in a group without counting. Subitizing is not the creation of an estimate or guess, but rather indicates that the person can visually determine the precise amount. As children play mathematics games consistently, they develop the ability to subitize frequent and familiar amounts, typically fewer than five.

Vignette for Understanding: Counting and Adding

Jon and Allysa are setting the table for lunch today. Each table needs to have four places set. Ms. Tina hands Jon a stack of eight plates and asks him if he can divide them into two equal groups of four and leave them on the table for Allysa to place. She watches closely as he counts—one, two, three, four—as he removes the plates one at a time from the stack. Allysa is walking around to each table holding a container with forks. "How many forks do we need today?" asks Ms. Tina. Allysa turns to count the number of children in the room. She carefully begins with herself, then Jon, and then the remaining children reading books in the class circle. Allysa counts seven children and, for confirmation, asks, "Ms. Tina, do we have seven children for lunch?" "We have seven right now," Ms. Tina explains, "but Nicole is coming later when her grandma drops her off. How many will we have when she joins us?" Allysa pauses and excitedly responds, "Eight!" Ms. Tina responds, "Great adding, Allysa."

Reflection

In this example, Ms. Tina turns a mundane experience into a math-rich learning opportunity. Posing questions and using materials to help provide support for the children's thinking are strategies that promote quantification skill development. These everyday quantification experiences let children practice the skills they were initially exposed to in formal mathematics lessons.

Planning Tips for Integrating Number Sense

Opportunities for exploration and integration of numbers and number sense can occur during every part of the school day. In the lessons and vignettes presented in this chapter, opportunities for learning with and from numbers can be seen during daily routines, music and movement experiences, whole-group learning, and individual explorations. You can enhance opportunities for children to count, add, subtract, and estimate by posing related questions and encouraging children to document and make their thinking visible.

Questions for Inquiry and Exploration

The following types of questions can be used to encourage guided-inquiry explorations in numbers and number sense:

- How many colors are you painting with today?

- Do you have more or fewer puzzle pieces than I do?

- How many chicken nuggets do I need to add to the three on your plate so that you have five?

- You are right, four plus one does equal five. Can you tell me how you figured that out?

- There are four of you and four tricycles. Do we have enough for each of you to ride one?

Lesson Ideas

Making Matches

Topic: One-to-one correspondence

Objective:

Working individually or taking turns in pairs or groups, children will seek out a match that corresponds to a picture of everyday objects found in their classroom.

Materials:

Minimum of twenty printed photographs of classroom objects (blocks, cars, dolls, art tools, and so on)

Lamination equipment

Overview:

This game can be played individually, in pairs, or in small groups. The children will match objects in the classroom with photo cards of those objects.

In preparation, print out photographs of classroom objects that the children can pick up and move. Start with no more than two objects on each photo. You will want to print the photos the same size and laminate them. Ideally, you should have at least twenty photos so that you can make a deck of cards with them.

Activity Steps:

1. Explain to the children that they will get a photo card of objects in the classroom. They will take the card and find the same number of actual objects. Then they will lay the card down with the objects next to it. Make sure the children have space to lay out their one-to-one matches.

2. Talk with the children about what it means to match objects. In particular, focus on talking about one-to-one matches. You can ask these types of questions: How many toy trucks do you see in this picture? We need to make a match for this picture. How many toy trucks do we need to find in our classroom to make a match for this picture?

3. Either demonstrate the matching process first for the children, or invite one or two children to do a practice round to demonstrate.

4. Give each child a photo card, and ask them to find matching objects in the classroom to place next to their cards.

Creative Investigations in Early Math

5. Discuss individually, in small groups, or as a whole class how the children found their matches. Let them think aloud about the processes they used.

Documentation:

Observe children's one-to-one object matches. Take anecdotal notes on the children's abilities to explore numbers and problem solve.

Extension Lessons:

This game can be modified in many ways as the children gain experience with one-to-one matches. The matches can be increased in number—making matches of three, four, and five. The game can be extended into other content areas—natural materials can be used for science explorations, and colors can be used for visual art explorations.

Number Grab Bag

Topic: Number recognition ranging from zero to twenty

Objective:

Children will correctly identify numbers ranging from zero to twenty.

Materials:

Foam numbers, magnetic numbers, or number cards from zero to twenty

Bag to hold the numbers

Creativity Skill:

Communication

Overview:

This is a simple game to play in a whole-group setting, with children sitting in a circle, to encourage number recognition. Depending on the experience the children have with numbers, you can start with zero to ten or add in numbers past twenty as needed. Once children have some experience counting concrete objects, it is important to include zero in your explorations of number because many children struggle to understand the concept that *zero* stands for no objects. Typically, older preschoolers have enough experience with number and number sense to support the inclusion of zero in activities such as this one.

Activity Steps:

1. Pull a number out of the bag, and show it to the children. Encourage the children to tell you what number they see. It is beneficial to encourage group responses as you start playing this game so that children who are just beginning to recognize numbers can benefit from their classmates' knowledge.

2. Invite the children to take turns pulling out a number and saying what the number is. Ask others not to shout out the answer so that each child can participate during his turn. Have the children pass the bag around the circle.

3. If a child gives an incorrect response, you can ask the child to rethink the answer and place the number back into the bag to be drawn again. You might do this in an encouraging way by saying something like this: "Let's think about that number some more. If you put it back in the bag, we can come back and talk about it again later."

Documentation:

Take anecdotal notes on the children's abilities to recognize the numbers ranging from zero to twenty.

Extension Lesson:

The complexity of the game can be increased by including larger numbers. Children who need more assistance might find it less stressful to play in pairs and take turns with a partner.

Number Web

Topic: Number recognition ranging from one to twenty

Objective:

Children will correctly identify numbers ranging from one to twenty.

Materials:

Number cards with a number from one to twenty written on one side and the same number of dots on the other side

Large ball of yarn

Digital camera (optional)

Overview:

This game is designed for a whole-group setting, with children sitting in a circle.

Activity Steps:

1. Shuffle the number cards, and place them in a stack. Pass the stack around the circle, asking each child to take the top card.

2. Tell the children that they will be asked to identify the number on their card, using the dots on the back of the card if needed.

3. Call out the number one. Hand the child with that card the end of the string on the ball of yarn, and ask her to hold onto it in one hand and hold onto the number card in the other hand.

4. Tell the children that they will need to stay where they are, and you will bring the ball of yarn to them.

5. Ask who has the number two. Unravel the yarn so that the child with the number two can hold onto it.

6. Continue calling out numbers in order until all of the children are holding the yarn.

7. Once this is complete, ask children to think about the web. Support their understanding with questions: Can you think of another type of web? Is each person connected to someone else?

8. Take a photo of the children holding the spiderweb to remind them of the process of connecting numbers.

Documentation:

Take anecdotal notes on the children's abilities to recognize the numbers ranging from one to twenty. The photo of the completed spiderweb can be displayed in the classroom as documentation.

Extension Lesson:

The complexity of the game can be increased by including larger numbers. You could start with the number ten, twenty, or thirty.

Jumping Numbers Game

Topic: Identifying numbers one to six

Objective:

Children will identify corresponding numbers to the numbers rolled on six-sided dice.

Materials:

Six-sided dot dice

Sidewalk chalk for outdoor spaces

Masking tape and a marker for indoor spaces

Creativity Skills:

Collaboration

Communication

Visualization

Overview:

This game combines physical activity and number sense. Prior to playing the game, create a horizontal number line and write the numbers one to six on the line. Make a box around each number—with chalk outside or with masking tape inside—that is large enough for a child to stand in. This game can be played individually, in pairs, or in small groups.

Activity Steps:

1. Before beginning play, talk with the children about the dice. Invite them to examine a die and see how each of the six faces shows a different number of dots. Ask them to count the number of dots on each side with you.

2. Have the children stand a few feet away from the number line.

3. Ask one child to roll a die and watch to see which side lands facing up. That is the number he will need to jump to on the number line and then stand in that box until the next number is rolled. If playing in small groups, the children will need to take turns rolling a die and counting.

4. Encourage the children to count together and help the player jump to the corresponding number on the number line.

Documentation:

Take anecdotal notes on the children's abilities to recognize and count one to six as well as cooperate with group members.

Extension Lessons:

The complexity of the game can be increased by having children roll two dice and add the numbers together to play with numbers one to twelve. You could also ask all players to count the number of jumps it takes for a child to reach the appropriate number box on the number line.

Number Puzzles

Topic: Identifying and ordering numbers from zero to twenty

Objective:

Children will identify and correctly place numbers ranging from zero to twenty to create a completed puzzle.

Materials:

8½" x 11" pieces of colored card stock

Ziplock bags for storing the pieces

Digital camera (optional)

Creativity Skills:

Problem solving

Visualization

Overview:

You will create numbered puzzle pieces for the children to fit together to complete a puzzle. The puzzles can be put together individually or in pairs.

Activity Steps:

1. Before introducing the activity to the children, label the paper with numbers in rows. If you want bigger puzzle pieces and a simpler game, use only zero to five on a piece of card stock. If you want smaller pieces and a more difficult game, you can label the piece of card stock with numbers up to twenty. Cut in between the numbers to create abstract, organic shapes so that the puzzle will fit together in only one way. Create one puzzle for each child or group.

2. Put all of the pieces for one puzzle in a ziplock bag. Label the bag with the largest number in the puzzle so that the children have an end point for counting.

3. Tell the children to each take a puzzle bag, and then have them put the pieces together.

4. Ask them to lay out the pieces on the table with the number side up. Encourage the children to think about what number comes next each time they place a puzzle piece.

5. Once the children have completed the puzzle, encourage them to count through all of the placed pieces to ensure that they have put the puzzle together correctly.

Documentation:

Take anecdotal notes on the children's abilities to recognize and count zero to twenty as well as cooperate with group members. Take photos of the children in the process of completing the puzzle as well as photos of the completed puzzle for a source of documentation that the children can revisit.

Extension Lessons:

You can make the puzzles increasingly complex by adding more numbers, which will result in smaller pieces to manipulate. You can also encourage children to create their own number puzzles.

Lining Up in Order

Topic: Using the ordinal numbers first through fifth

Objective:

Children will use the ordinal numbers first through fifth to describe the position of children in a line.

Materials:

Masking tape

Index cards

Overview:

This activity gives children practice putting things in a specified order. Before beginning the activity, place five pieces of masking tape on the floor or tape five index cards down in a line for the children to stand on.

> **Creativity Skills:**
>
> Collaboration
>
> Communication
>
> Problem solving

Activity Steps:

1. In a whole-group setting, introduce the children to the term *ordinal numbers* and use the terms *first, second, third, fourth,* and *fifth* to describe the placement of children next to you in the circle or in rows.

2. Compare and contrast the ordinal number words with counting numbers. Talk about how counting numbers, or cardinal numbers, are used to tell how many, but ordinal numbers are used to show us the position of something. Explain that the first child next to you in the circle is in the first position.

3. Invite five children to stand up, and ask them to order or position themselves in a line saying, "Thomas will line up first. Jaxon will line up second behind Thomas…."

4. Once the children are lined up, ask other students to identify who is in the first position, second position, third position, and so on. Encourage children to use the ordinal numbers in their responses.

5. Repeat the experience with the remaining groups of children until everyone has had at least one turn.

Documentation:

Take anecdotal notes on the children's abilities to use ordinal numbers to describe relative positions.

Extension Lessons:

You can extend this activity to any everyday experience that calls for children to line up or position themselves around a table. Additional ordinal numbers through the size of the class can be added as children gain experience and understanding of *first* through *fifth*.

To extend and shift this lesson to group counting experiences, the children can count the different colors of clothing that members of the class are wearing, the days in the month, the days until a big event, or various objects from one to twenty.

You can also engage the children in singing counting songs:

"Five Green and Speckled Frogs"

Five green and speckled frogs
Sat on a speckled log
Eating some most delicious bugs.
Yum, yum!

One jumped into the pool,
Where it was nice and cool.
Then there were four green speckled frogs.
Glub, glub.

[Continue on, reducing the number.]

Four green and speckled frogs...
Three green and speckled frogs...
Two green and speckled frogs...
One green and speckled frog...
...Then there were no green speckled frogs!
Glub, glub, glub, glub.

Creative Investigations in Early Math

"Ten in the Bed"

There were ten in the bed,
And the little one said,
"Roll over! Roll over!"
So they all rolled over and one fell out.

Then there were just 1, 2, 3, 4, 5, 6, 7, 8

Nine in the bed,
And the little one said,
"Roll over! Roll over!"
So they all rolled over and one fell out.

[Continue on, reducing the number.]

Then there was just one in the bed,
And the little one said,
"Hey! Where did everybody go?"

Children's Books

Blackstone, Stella. 2005. *My Granny Went to Market: A Round-the-World Counting Rhyme*. Cambridge, Mass.: Barefoot Books.

>   This multicultural counting book features a grandmother who travels around the world buying items unique to each location.

Cronin, Doreen. 2006. *Click, Clack, Splish, Splash: A Counting Adventure*. New York: Atheneum Books for Young Readers.

>   This engaging, introductory book—part of the *Click, Clack, Moo* series—covers counting from one to ten.

Johnson, Stephen T. 2003. *City by Numbers*. New York: Puffin Books.

>   Using real-life photographs, this book challenges children to identify numbers one to twenty-one in urban scenes.

3
Computation

Young children are quick to notice when the number of items in a collection of desired objects is decreasing or increasing. Ensuring the fair distribution of a limited amount of toys or materials is a frequent theme among preschoolers. To develop an understanding of computation, children need many opportunities to match and count objects.

Specific computation skills noted in the NCTM standards can be introduced in early childhood classrooms through scaffolded, intentional learning experiences. Concrete modeling of addition involves using manipulatives or materials to add two sets of objects together; likewise, modeling of subtraction should involve the use of manipulatives or concrete items to demonstrate how objects can be taken away from a group. Equal division involves opportunities to share or split a group of objects equally. The counting-on strategy is another important computation skill that involves being able to continue counting on from a number other than one when adding sets of objects together.

Using the language of mathematics is an important part of the process of understanding computation. Natural opportunities to use computation words, including the following terms, occur frequently throughout the day:

addition	counting on
equals	minus
number	plus
subtraction	set
sum	take away

Number and Operations

Compute fluently and make reasonable estimates

In pre-K through grade 2 all students should—

- develop and use strategies for whole-number computations, with a focus on addition and subtraction;

- develop fluency with basic number combinations for addition and subtraction;

- use a variety of methods and tools to compute, including objects, mental computation, estimation, paper and pencil, and calculators.

Source: National Council of Teachers of Mathematics. 2000. *Principles and Standards for School Mathematics.* Reston, VA: NCTM. Reproduced with permission.

Vignette for Understanding: Computation in the Classroom

Four children are gathered around the math table, ready to play a new board game that involves each child getting three colored counters to use in marking his progress in the game. There are twelve counters in all. Mr. Baker asks the children to look at the pile of counters and decide how they will distribute them so that each child gets the needed amount. Micah suggests that the group make four different piles out of the larger pile. Tomi suggests that they can take turns taking a counter until they are all gone. Mr. Baker says, "Great ideas. We can divide up the big pile into four groups, or we can all take turns picking up a counter until we each get to three. Which would you like to try?" The children decide to take turns taking counters from the bigger pile one at a time until there are no more counters in the center pile. Once they successfully complete their task and each of the four children has three counters, Mr. Baker says, "Great job counting out four equal sets. I'd like for us to try Micah's strategy now. Can you put your counters back in a big pile just for a minute? Then Micah can show us what he was thinking." Micah looks at the big pile and slowly counts out three to take away, creating his first pile and then repeating the action three more times. "Great job, Micah!" Mr. Baker adds, "Did you all notice Micah's strategy? He took away three from the big pile of twelve so that he could make each group." Dani comments, "Both ways made four groups of three counters."

Reflection

While working with the children, Mr. Baker encouraged them to pose possible strategies for solving the problem. He also encouraged the children to work the problem in different ways to explore the strategies posed by his students. Practicing problem solving in different ways will help to support children's flexible use and understanding of number and computation. Mr. Baker also encouraged the use of mathematics language throughout the experience by using words such as *equal*, *set*, and *take away*.

Planning Tips for Integrating Computation

Opportunities to engage in *computational thinking*—the ability to recognize change in sets or collections when objects are added to or taken away from the groups—are unlimited in an early childhood classroom. As young children engage with materials and media in the classroom, they naturally begin to group objects into sets and explore notions of which group has more or less, or if they have equal amounts. As you plan lessons in the visual arts with arts materials or in science with natural objects, opportunities will arise to encourage children to group, count, and modify sets. Staying tuned in to how children are making sense out of objects and materials will help to show when teacher questioning can be helpful in extending student thinking. For example, it is not uncommon to see a preschooler double count an object or skip an object while counting a set of items. If you notice this happening, it can be helpful to ask the child to count out the set again with you while you model physically touching each item as it is counted. By touching each item during counting, you are providing the child with a strategy that she can use independently to support her understanding of number and computation.

Questions for Inquiry and Exploration

The following questions provide examples of how you can encourage guided-inquiry explorations in computation:

- Which group has more? How do you know?

- If we wanted to divide these items into two equal groups, what could we do?

- If you have four puppets and you share one with Marcus, how may puppets will you still have?

- How many do you have? How many do I have? Who has more?

Lesson Ideas

More or Fewer

Topic: Comparing groups of items to numbers on cards, and deciding which has more or fewer, or if they are the same

Objectives:

Children will count groups with no more than five items.

Children will use number words as they count.

Children will compare groups using the words *more*, *fewer*, or *equal* to explain their comparisons.

Materials:

Cards with the numbers one to five displayed in numerals and dots

Several groups of five objects, such as counting bears, buttons, or colored counters

Creativity Skills:

Collaboration

Communication

Problem solving

Overview:

In this introductory lesson, children will play along with you as you create a grouping of objects and ask them to compare the number of objects to different number cards.

Activity Steps:

1. Create a group of objects of between one and five items.

2. Shuffle the number cards and put them in a stack.

3. Pull a number card from one to five, and ask the children if the card or the group has more. For example, if three counting bears are in a group and you pull out the number card with one, then the intent is for the children to recognize that the group has more.

4. Repeat the question for all five cards. If the card and group have the same number, then the children can say that they are equal.

5. Following that exchange, repeat the game with the following question: Which has fewer, the card or the group?

6. The game can be repeated until each child becomes proficient and accurate when responding.

Documentation:

Take anecdotal notes on children's abilities to count items and compare groups.

Extension Lesson:

The concepts of *more*, *fewer*, and *equal* can be extended by including larger numbers and asking children to play in pairs.

How Many?

Topic: Count and document the number of a specific type of item in the everyday environment

Objectives:

Children will count and document the number of everyday items in their classroom or school.

Children will use number words as they count.

Children will compare groups of objects looking for similarities and differences.

Children will use descriptive words (such as *more*, *less*, *greater*, *fewer*, *same*, and *equal*) to explain their comparisons.

Materials:

Student math journals or plain paper

Crayons, markers, or pencils

Creativity Skills:

Collaboration

Communication

Documentation

Problem solving

Overview:

This activity helps children become comfortable with counting and recognizing that they can practice and have fun counting items anywhere they go. You can plan this activity for the whole class, small groups, or individuals.

Activity Steps:

1. Explain to the children that they will be counting the numbers of specific objects in their classroom or school and will use their math journal to document what they find.

2. For practice, encourage the children to count the number of windows in their classroom. They can document the number of windows they find by drawing a window or writing the word *window* in their math journal and writing the corresponding number next to the word or drawing.

3. You can suggest a few items for the children to count, and then let them choose items on their own.

4. Talk with the children about comparing, or looking for similarities and differences. Then ask the children to compare some of the items they have counted. Some questions to consider: Do we have more doors or windows in our classroom? What do we have equal numbers of in our classroom? How can you tell they are the same amount?

5. Introduce and reinforce the math vocabulary for the children during the game: *more, less, fewer, greater, same*, and *equal*.

Documentation:

Children's math journals can be used as an informal measure of understanding.

Building On

Topic: Gain experience recognizing numerals and number words, and count a number of items to add on

Objectives:

Children will recognize both the numeral and corresponding number word from one to ten.

Children will be able to count out a specified number of blocks to add to a structure.

Materials:

Small or large building blocks

Number cards with numerals and number words for one to ten

Creativity Skills:

Collaboration

Communication

Opportunities for unique problem solving

Strategic planning

Overview:

This game will require small groups of children to work together to build a collaborative block structure.

Activity Steps:

1. Create groups of two to three children.

2. Explain that the objective of this game is to see how large of a structure they can build together.

3. Ask children to take turns drawing a card from the deck and then adding the number of blocks specified on the card to the group's structure.

4. Encourage group members to count together as one member adds blocks at each turn.

5. If the structure falls or collapses, the group can begin again.

Documentation:

Take anecdotal notes on the children's abilities to collaborate, solve problems, recognize and use numerals and number words, and count.

Extension Lessons:

You can add cards with larger numbers as children gain experience with the numbers and the game. Increase the variety of shapes and colors of blocks to increase the complexity of the game.

Comparing Groups

Topic: Compare groups of matched objects and describe the groups using math language

Objectives:

Children will compare groups of objects looking for similarities and differences.

Children will use descriptive words (*more, less, greater, fewer, same,* and *equal*) to explain their comparisons.

Materials:

A variety of counting materials (colored cubes, leaves, seashells, and so on)

Student math journals or plain paper

Crayons, markers, or pencils

Creativity Skills:

Collaboration

Communication

Documentation

Problem solving

Visualization

Overview:

Children will work in small groups to set up, count, and compare different groups of five or fewer items. This activity is designed to encourage children to count and compare sets of similar and different items. It is best to play this game the first time with items that are similar. You can introduce the grouping of different kinds of items once children have experience and understand the basic premise of the game. For example, if you begin by using counting bears, children can create two groupings of bears. The next time they play the game, you can invite them to create groupings with materials of different shapes, sizes, and colors, which will challenge their comparison skills as they count through the items.

Activity Steps:

1. Discuss with the children what it means to compare one group of items, or set, to another.

2. Explain that you will have leaders and counters. Leaders will create sets of items of five or fewer. Counters will decide whether the sets have the same or different number of items. Invite children to take turns in their small group until each one has had a chance to be a leader and a counter.

3. Ask the children to use their math journals or blank paper to document each round of their game. Encourage the children to draw or write—using whatever methods are appropriate based on their individual literacy skills. For example, they could draw a picture of a bear counter and then write the number next to it. Or they could write the word *bear* in addition to the picture.

4. Introduce and reinforce the math vocabulary for the children during the game using the words *more, less, fewer, greater, same,* and *equal.*

5. If this is the children's first time playing this game, you can do a few practice rounds together. Some questions to consider: How can you tell if these two groups have the same amount? What can you do to test that idea? Let's count them together. Are they equal or does one group have more?

Documentation:

Take anecdotal notes on the children's abilities to collaborate, solve problems, visualize, and compare and contrast groups. Review child-created journal pages for additional documentation.

Extension Lesson:

As the children demonstrate proficiency in counting and comparing items in groups, the children can create groups of more than five items.

Adding to the Story

Topic: Computation through storytelling

Objectives:

Children will participate in a group storytelling experience.

Children will describe changes that occur in a group when more objects are added to a group or combined together.

Children will describe changes that occur in a group when objects are taken away or separated from the group.

Creativity Skills:

Collaboration

Communication

Exploration

Problem solving

Visualization

Materials:

Large drawing paper

Colored pencils and fine-tipped markers

Felt board with felt characters (optional)

Whiteboard and dry-erase markers (optional)

Overview:

Introduce the concept of a group storytelling experience. Talk with the children about how they will work together to create a story. The children can add to the story using their imaginations, but they will need to be respectful of others during this experience. Taking turns will help support the group experience by ensuring that each child has a chance to engage in storytelling.

Activity Steps:

1. Start the activity by drawing a character or a few characters on drawing paper or a whiteboard, or using felt characters on a felt board. Ask the children to count how many characters are shown.

2. Begin to tell the story, and then ask a child to share what happens next.

3. If this is a first-time experience, it can help the children to begin with a familiar story and modify it as the activity moves along. A story such as "The Three Little Pigs" or "Snow White and the Seven Dwarves" can provide an easy starting point because groups of objects are central to these stories. For example, you could begin "The Three Little Pigs" by drawing the pigs or using felt characters. Ask the children to count the pigs. You could change up the familiar story by adding in two piggy cousins to the story's cast of characters. Draw two new characters to add to the group of three. Ask the children to count the number of pigs again.

4. Emphasize the mathematics language of *more* and *fewer*. Continue with the story. Invite children to add in new characters or remove characters from the story in their storytelling. Be sure to pause the story where necessary to conduct a new character count.

Documentation:

Take anecdotal notes on the children's ability to collaborate, solve problems, and visualize. Use the storyboard as a means to document the numbers of characters and the problems encountered in the story.

Counting On

Topic: Use a zero-to-ten number line to find the sum of a number puzzle

Objective:

Children will use the number line to count on to a given number.

Materials:

At least twenty unruled, 4" x 6" index cards

Marker

Number line from zero to ten

A colored counter or small item to support counting

Overview:

As this activity involves new ideas and procedures, it is best to introduce this lesson to the children in either a whole- or small-group setting. Children will count along the number line and leave the counter at the end number, and then they will add on while using the counter. Counting on or counting up from a number is an important mental math strategy. It will take the children time to learn because they are used to beginning all counting at the number one.

Activity Steps:

1. In advance, prepare the index cards by drawing a vertical line in the middle of each one on the front side. Write a numeral on each side of the line, choosing numbers that together add up to ten or less. For example: 5 | 3; 4 | 2. On the back side of each card, write the sum of the two numbers that appear on the front of the card. Put the cards in a pile, with the front side up.

2. Begin by showing the children the number line and having them count out the numbers from one to ten together. Tell the children that they will be using the number line to help them solve number problems.

3. Explain to the children that they will play this game by taking a card from the pile and counting to the first number shown on the front

Creative Investigations in Early Math

of the card. Then they will use the second number on the front of the card and count on from the first number.

4. Tell the children that you will do a sample problem together. Take a problem card from the pile, and have the children tell you the first number on the card. Using your colored counter, count out the first number on the number line.

5. Explain that you will be using the second number to count on from the first number. Demonstrate for the children. You might say, "Our first number was five, and you can see my counter is now on the number five. The second number is three, so I need to count on from five." As you move the counter, count the numbers out loud. "What number is my counter on? Yes, eight! When we have five and count on three more, we end up with the number eight. Let's turn the card over to see if we are correct." Show the children the sum on the back of the card.

6. In order to best scaffold this lesson, play alongside the children several times until they feel comfortable taking on the challenges individually or in pairs.

7. When they are ready to play on their own, ask them to take turns drawing a card, counting to the first number, and counting on from there to reach the sum of the two numbers.

Documentation:

Take anecdotal notes on the children's abilities to count as they respond to the counting-on problems.

Extension Lessons:

As children gain experience with the number line and the concept of counting on, encourage them to draw number lines in their math journals and create their own number puzzles to solve.

For group time, you and the children can create groups and compare them. Pose questions to the children about what happens when you add or take away items in a given set.

Children's Books

Baker, Keith. 2004. *Quack and Count.* Orlando, FL: Voyager.
    Follow along as seven ducklings are grouped into various combinations during their daily adventures.

Giganti, Paul, Jr. 1992. *Each Orange Had 8 Slices: A Counting Book.* New York: Greenwillow.
    Vibrant artwork illustrates math puzzles involving everyday objects that children can work to solve as they listen to the story.

Sayre, April Pulley, and Jeff Sayre. 2006. *One Is a Snail, Ten Is a Crab.* Cambridge, MA: Candlewick.
    Using the feet of various animals, children can explore number sets up to one hundred.

4
Geometry and Spatial Sense

Exploring geometry and spatial sense is an important component of early mathematics learning. Young children build their understanding of shapes when they engage in experiences that invite them to move and manipulate shapes. As children build with blocks or play with math manipulatives such as tangrams, they will encounter times when they will need to maneuver these items to create their work. Learning to slide, turn, and flip items is important to building an understanding of spatial sense and transformations. Preschoolers will enjoy exploring the concepts of *shape, size, position, directionality,* and *motion*. As they develop their spatial sense, children learn to compare and manipulate mental images. Young children build their spatial awareness by understanding themselves in relation to the objects in their environment.

As young children explore shapes, play with puzzles, and make maps of their surroundings, they are building visual-reasoning skills, investigating the attributes of geometric figures, and building knowledge about two- and three-dimensional objects. Learning in these areas also supports the development of arithmetic skills and carries over into social studies, language arts, science, and the arts. For example, taking a class walk to find shapes in the environment—the window is shaped as a square, and the stop sign is shaped as an octagon—connects children to their immediate community in a way that can build on social studies experiences; likewise, an understanding of spatial sense is important to the visual and performing arts as children draw scenery or dance with peers.

When planning activities involving geometry and spatial sense, consider the relevant guidance and standards provided by NCTM:

Geometry

Analyze characteristics and properties of two- and three-dimensional geometric shapes and develop mathematical arguments about geometric relationships

In pre-K through grade 2 all students should—

- recognize, name, build, draw, compare, and sort two- and three-dimensional shapes;

- describe attributes and parts of two- and three-dimensional shapes;

- investigate and predict the results of putting together and taking apart two- and three-dimensional shapes.

Specify locations and describe spatial relationships using coordinate geometry and other representational systems

In pre-K through grade 2 all students should—

- describe, name, and interpret relative positions in space and apply ideas about relative position;

- describe, name, and interpret direction and distance in navigating space and apply ideas about direction and distance;

- find and name locations with simple relationships such as "near to" and in coordinate systems such as maps.

Apply transformations and use symmetry to analyze mathematical situations

In pre-K through grade 2 all students should—

- recognize and apply slides, flips, and turns;

- recognize and create shapes that have symmetry.

Creative Investigations in Early Math

Use visualization, spatial reasoning, and geometric modeling to solve problems

In pre-K through grade 2 all students should—

- create mental images of geometric shapes using spatial memory and spatial visualization;

- recognize and represent shapes from different perspectives;

- relate ideas in geometry to ideas in number and measurement;

- recognize geometric shapes and structures in the environment and specify their location.

Source: National Council of Teachers of Mathematics. 2000. *Principles and Standards for School Mathematics.* Reston, VA: NCTM. Reproduced with permission.

Properties of Shapes

From infancy, children experience a variety of shapes in their everyday environments. Windows are squares, doors are rectangles, bowls are circles, and pizza slices are triangles. As children experience their environment, they begin to understand how shapes can be combined and recombined in many different ways. Early experiences with shapes help children to describe, classify, build, and reconstruct the world around them.

Two-Dimensional Shapes

- They are flat and can be drawn or printed on paper or other flat surfaces.

- They have two dimensions: length and width.

- They are known as *plane shapes*.

- A square is an example of a 2-D shape with four sides of the same length and four 90-degree angles.

Three-Dimensional Shapes

- These shapes are solid or hollow.
- They have three dimensions: length, width, and height.
- A cube is an example of a 3-D shape that has six square faces of the same size.

Vignette for Understanding: Photographing a Shape Walk

A small group of four-year-olds with digital cameras descend on their playground with the goal of locating and capturing images of various shapes. The children are taking part in a series of lessons on the properties of shapes, and today's lesson takes the form of a shape walk. The children and their teacher, Ms. Morgan, are slowly making their way around the common areas of the school looking for various shapes and then capturing the images with their cameras. As the children enter the playground, they move in various directions finding circles, squares, and rectangles. Ms. Morgan moves quickly between the children, exploring the images they have captured and asking questions such as, "How do you know that's a rectangle?" The children are also quick to share their images with friends—common images of circles and rare images of triangles. As the children slow their playground explorations, Ms.

The children spotted colorful circles on the playground.

The children noticed squares and rectangles when they looked up at the school building.

Morgan states that the shape walk will continue as the children move down the preschool hallway on their way back to their classroom. She reminds the children to continue to take pictures of the shapes they see along the way for use in their classroom documentation.

Reflection

Taking the time to ask guiding questions, as Ms. Morgan did during the shape walk, serves to extend and bring meaning to geometric experiences and lessons. Naming and recognizing the attributes of geometric figures—square, circle, triangle, rectangle, rhombus, pentagon, octagon, and hexagon—is an important foundational skill and helps to build emerging understandings of the properties of shapes. The shape-walk experience along with Ms. Morgan's questioning and conversation about the children's images, offered many opportunities for the children to openly explore and learn from and with their teacher and peers. This learning experience also encouraged both critical thinking and the sharing of ideas—two skills that are central to inquiry learning and creative thinking.

Spatial Relationships

As children gain experience in recognizing and naming various shapes, they will use that knowledge to build understandings about the relationship between and among objects. When learning about spatial relationships, children explore the concept of where they or objects are in relation to another object or person. This exploration of relationships can help them develop spatial visualization and orientation skills. Young children's spatial skills will help them build understandings of the shape, size, and position of various objects. *Spatial orientation* involves the location of an object and requires children to use and understand positional words such as *above*, *below*, *outside*, and *inside*. *Spatial visualization* is the ability to generate, manipulate, and transform shapes in one's mind, which involves problem-solving and creativity skills. You can support these emerging spatial relationship skills through rich experiences exploring the everyday environments of the home, school, and playground settings.

Vignette for Understanding: The Dragon and Position Words

A small group of five-year-olds is gathered around a table to join their teacher, Ms. Roberts, for an integrated math and literacy lesson. Ms. Roberts announces that today the group will need to work together to create a story using a special set of math words. She says, "These words are called position words. Have you ever heard of the word position before?" Several children quickly say they have. Ms. Roberts invites Kimberly to share her ideas with the group. Kimberly responds, "I know position means like a place. Like a place in line." "Exactly!" replies Ms. Roberts, "Think about when we line up. Your friend might be behind you. Behind is a position word. It helps us understand where something is located."

Ms. Roberts goes on to introduce a list of four position words—*above*, *below*, *up*, and *down*—that the group will be working with that day. After some discussion of what each word means and how to determine the position of an object, the children begin working on a story together that uses each of the four words. Teyvon develops the first sentence, setting the tone for the group's story. "The dragon lives above the people on top of a huge mountain." Ms. Roberts carefully writes Teyvon's sentence on a large piece of paper on the table in front of the group. The children and Ms. Roberts develop the following sentence to build on Teyvon's description of the scene. "The town below the dragon's mountain has a lot of buildings." Kristin struggles to add a sentence to the story and offers, "The people never go up to the dragon's home because it is so high." Kimberly decides the last line of the story should read, "The dragon comes down to the town when he gets hungry, and the people leave him food."

Ms. Roberts reads the story aloud for the group and they decide they like what they have created. She goes on to explain that the group members now have an important task—they will need to create a drawing that depicts the story they developed together. She invites them to refer to the story and list of position words to help them with their story drawing. The children quickly begin working on their story pictures as they talk about the adventures of the dragon.

Teyvon drew a picture of the dragon story.

Reflection

In Ms. Roberts's classroom, the geometric lesson of introducing position words was seamlessly integrated with the language arts and visual arts content areas. The children had opportunities to work together in small groups, learn from and with each other, and demonstrate their understanding of the position words in their individual work. The combination of small-group and individual work times can allow teachers to observe and document children's levels of understanding during authentic learning experiences.

Language and Position Words

Natural opportunities to use position words occur frequently in early childhood classrooms as children engage in block-building experiences with their peers. When children understand descriptive position words, they can use them to promote cooperation as they build with other children.

In addition to block play, preschoolers may enjoy making maps to learn about spatial relationships. When children draw maps, they are tasked with thinking about the location of elements they want to display on the drawing. Maps provide further opportunities to use position words when describing location, which is an important mathematical idea. Maps also help children learn about the concept of *direction*. Simple drawings of the classroom, playground, and other areas where a child has sustained, daily interactions can be used to develop emerging understandings of location and direction and provide opportunities to use the following position words:

above	below	up
down	top	bottom
right	left	side
beside	through	on
over	under	inside
outside		

Symmetry and Motion

Young children use geometric motions naturally when they solve puzzles and build with blocks. Watch as they turn, flip, and slide each piece into place. As they explore through motion, they also gain experience with symmetry. For example, they learn that a square block has four equal sides or that a piece of paper cut into a circle can be folded down the center to create a half circle, or semicircle. These types of explorations help children understand position and object orientation.

Vignette for Understanding: Symmetric Play

As Grayson's class is preparing for rest time, the children are playing quietly or looking at books. Grayson invites Mrs. Pratt to play a favorite shape game. He brings over the glass cabochons from the art area, spreads them on the floor, and announces, "I'm going to go first. You have to guess and see if you know what the shape will be." He carefully places his first four gems into a diamond shape. Mrs. Pratt watches and mimics his movements to create her own mirror shape. "It looks like a diamond right now," she states. Grayson continues to build out his shape, adding more cabochons carefully to expand the original shape. Grayson and Mrs. Pratt work side by side for several minutes and spend time comparing their shapes to ensure that they are identical. Once they are satisfied with the mirror images they have created, they push the cabochons together into a pile. This time Mrs. Pratt takes the lead to create a new shape, and Grayson mimics her movements.

The child and teacher strive to position their play pieces to form mirror images.

Reflection

Grayson and Mrs. Pratt worked together to create two separate, but mirror-image figures. An important element of geometry—specifically spatial visualization—is the ability to engage in shape transformations, including making them symmetrical, rotating them, and flipping them. A shape is symmetrical when it can be divided into two identical pieces. Similarly, when a shape is flipped over a line, it can produce its own mirror image. When an object is rotated 360 degrees on a rotational point, it will return to its original position. Simple activities, such as Grayson and Mrs. Pratt's game with symmetry, can build foundational understanding for the concepts of *line* and *shape*, which are important to understanding the concept of *symmetry*. The use of open-ended, loose-part materials allowed Grayson to create shapes from memory, as the materials did not dictate the creation of a particular shape or figure. Open-ended exploration and design are important aspects of a creative-learning experience.

Planning Tips for Integrating Geometry

Geometry and spatial sense can be integrated across many content areas in structured and unstructured experiences in ways that invite children to develop creative thinking and inquiry skills. In the lessons and vignettes presented in this chapter, there are many opportunities to integrate geometry, social studies, language arts, and the visual arts. Planning curricular experiences using a cross-disciplinary approach encourages teachers to explore the overlapping skills, concepts, and attitudes in multiple disciplines. As an example, asking children to make a map of their bedroom at home promotes the geometric ideas of *location* and *direction* while also serving as a bridge to home-school connections and social studies experiences.

Questions for Inquiry and Exploration

The following are a brief listing of questions that can be used to encourage guided-inquiry explorations in geometry:

- How do you know this shape is a triangle?

- Is that shape the same as this one? How are they the same? How are they different?

- What shape could you make if you combined these shapes?

- Have you ever seen a shape like this before? Where?

- Would your shape roll? Bounce? Stack on top of others?

- What would we need to do to change this square into a rectangle? Circle into an oval?

- How can you use the scissors to cut this square into a triangle? What will you need to cut away?

Lesson Ideas

Reproducing Shapes

Topic: Introduction to circles, triangles, rectangles, and squares

Objectives:

Children will create circles, triangles, rectangles, and squares.

Children will name circles, triangles, rectangles, and squares.

Materials:

Sand or shaving cream

Individual trays

Construction paper or card stock shapes—circles, triangles, rectangles, and squares—in various sizes

Digital camera (optional)

Creativity Skills:

Exploration

Visualization

Overview:

As both sand and shaving cream are used frequently in the classroom, this exploratory lesson will build on that familiarity and let children use their fingers to create circles, triangles, rectangles, and squares. Please note that children will likely want to freely explore the sand or shaving cream before and during this lesson, which is an appropriate and important part of their exploration.

Activity Steps:

1. In advance, prepare a tray with sand or shaving cream for each child.

2. Show the children the construction paper shapes, and invite them to name the shapes if they can. Introduce the name of each shape and talk about the properties of the different shapes.

3. Lay out the example shapes on the tables where the children can see them. Tell the children that they will be looking at the shapes and that they can draw their own shapes in the sand or shaving cream on their own trays.

4. Invite the children to draw the shapes with their fingers, and encourage them to talk with the other children at their tables about what shapes they have drawn.

5. As children are engaging with the materials, pose questions and work alongside them. You can support their inquiry by asking them if they can make certain shapes, what certain shapes are, and how they knew what the shapes were. Offer encouragement, and remind the children to name the shapes they make and see.

6. Remember that the children do not need to stay focused only on shape making. Making other marks allows them to use creativity and imagination and will help them develop fine motor skills.

Documentation:

Take anecdotal notes on the children's abilities to create and recognize circles, triangles, rectangles, and squares. You can also photograph the children's trays as a source of documentation.

Extension Lesson:

Encourage children to create shapes as they draw on paper and use the correct names for the shapes they create.

Guessing Shapes

Topic: Recognizing and describing the attributes of a circle, triangle, rectangle, oval, hexagon, and square

Objectives:

Children will describe how shapes are similar and different.

Children will recognize and name these two-dimensional shapes: circle, triangle, rectangle, oval, hexagon, and square.

Materials:

Construction paper or card stock circles, triangles, rectangles, ovals, hexagons, and squares in various sizes

Bag to hold the shape cutouts

Creativity Skills:

Collaboration

Communication

Exploration

Opportunities for unique problem solving

Visualization

Overview:

This shape-guessing game can be introduced during a whole-group lesson and then played by children in small groups once they understand the goals of the game.

Activity Steps:

1. Introduce any shapes you have not already discussed with the children. Make sure you have examples of all of the shapes displayed where the children can see them. Go over the names and attributes of all of the shapes. It is helpful to revisit this information as a group to prompt the children's memory without putting them on the spot to recall information individually.

2. Explain to the children that you will pass around a bag filled with shapes, and one child will pull a shape out of the bag and keep it hidden from the group. The class will ask questions one at a time to try to guess the shape that the child is holding.

3. Model a question or two to get the children started. You might ask some of the following questions: How many corners does the shape have? Is the shape round? Does the shape have four sides that are all the same? Does the shape have four sides that look different?

4. The child that names the correct shape gets to choose a shape out of the shape bag next, and the questioning continues.

5. Collect the correctly identified shapes so that the children will stay focused on each new shape drawn out of the bag.

Documentation:

Take anecdotal notes on the children's abilities to recognize the different two-dimensional shapes and their abilities to describe the attributes of the shapes.

Extension Lessons:

As the children gain experience with 2-D shapes, add 3-D shapes to the game to increase complexity and extend the learning.

Encourage children to collaborate and make simple shapes with their bodies.

3-D Shape Modeling

Topic: Introduction to three-dimensional shapes: cube, prism, cylinder, pyramid, sphere, and cone

Objectives:

Children will describe how 3-D shapes are similar and different.

Children will recognize and name these 3-D shapes: cube, prism, cylinder, pyramid, sphere, and cone.

Materials:

Variety of small- and medium-size 3-D shape blocks

Modeling clay or playdough

Overview:

As playdough and modeling clay are a regular part of creative-arts experiences in the classroom, this exploratory lesson will build on that familiarity and introduce several 3-D shapes: cube, prism, cylinder, pyramid, sphere, and cone. Please note that children might want to freely explore the modeling clay or playdough before and during this lesson, which is fine.

Activity Steps:

1. Introduce each 3-D shape by showing the children the shape blocks. Ask them to name the shapes if they can. Talk about the name of each shape and the shape's properties.

2. Put blocks of each shape on the tables where the children can see them.

3. Invite children to use the clay or playdough to make some of the shapes. Encourage the children to name the shapes they make and see.

4. As the children are engaging with the materials, pose questions and work alongside them. You might ask some of the following types of questions: Can you make a sphere by rolling the clay between your hands? What shape is this? How did you know that was a cube? Does the cone I made look like a birthday hat?

5. Remember that the children do not need to stay focused only on shape making. Allow them to freely explore the properties of the sculpting media to encourage creativity, imagination, and development of fine motor skills.

Documentation:

Take anecdotal notes on the children's abilities to recognize the different 3-D shapes and to describe the attributes of shapes.

Extension Lesson:

As the children gain experience with 3-D shapes, encourage them to think about and create different objects using a shape as a base. For example, a cube becomes the foundation of a house, and a cylinder becomes the body of a dog. Give them opportunities to build onto their shapes in creative ways.

2-D to 3-D Shape Making

Topic: Recognize how two-dimensional shapes form the basis of three-dimensional shapes

Objectives:

Children will recognize triangles, rectangles, hexagons, and squares, and name these 2-D shapes.

Children will recognize cubes, prisms, and pyramids, and name these 3-D shapes.

Children will recognize the 2-D shapes that make up the sides of the 3-D shapes.

Materials:

Variety of small- and medium-size 3-D shape blocks

Modeling clay

Toothpicks

Digital camera (optional)

Creativity Skills:

Exploration

Opportunities for unique problem solving

Strategic planning

Visualization

Overview:

In this lesson, children will create 2-D shapes with toothpicks and clay. Each child will then add to his 2-D shape, which can form the starting point for the 3-D shape. Squares form the base of a cube and of a square pyramid. Triangles form the sides of a pyramid and the ends of a triangular prism. Rectangles form the sides of a triangular prism. This experience involves multiple steps and experimentation, so it is best if you work alongside the children in small groups of three or four to offer support and encouragement.

Activity Steps:

1. As you support children's efforts during this activity, explain the following terms related to 3-D shapes:

   • The *base* forms the bottom of the 3-D shape and supports the structure.

   • *Faces* are the flat parts of the shape.

   • *Edges* are the lines where two faces meet.

   • *Vertices* are the points where two or more edges meet.

2. Encourage the children to begin by making fifteen to twenty small clay balls (approximately 2 centimeters in diameter). For safety reasons, make sure the balls are not small enough to be choking hazards. Each child will need enough clay balls to create multiple shapes. The balls will connect the toothpicks, which form the shapes. For example, a child will need four toothpicks to form the edges of a square and four clay balls to connect the vertices of the toothpicks. When making a cube from a square, a child will need a total of twelve toothpicks and eight clay balls.

3. Ask each child to pick a 3-D shape to create. Once a shape is chosen, ask each child what 2-D shape looks like part of the 3-D shape. Encourage the children to use the 3-D shape blocks to support their thinking.

4. Once they have determined the 3-D shape, they are ready to begin creating the 2-D shape. As they build on the 2-D shape, they will need your help holding pieces in place until the sides of the shape support the weight of the piece.

Documentation:

The child's completed shape can serve as a form of documentation if allowed to dry. Photographs of the completed shapes can also serve as documentation. Take anecdotal notes on the children's abilities to recognize the 2-D shapes that make up faces of the 3-D shapes.

Extension Lesson:

This lesson can be done with children working in pairs to create shapes together, which will increase opportunities for problem solving and cooperation.

3-D Building: What Does Your House Look Like?

Topic: Learning to cooperate while planning and building structures using 3-D shape blocks

Objectives:

Children will name and discuss a variety of shapes, and they will note the shapes' similarities and differences.

Children will work together to construct a house out of a variety of shapes.

Materials:

Variety of small- and medium-size 3-D shape blocks

Clipboards

Pencils

Digital camera

Teacher-created checklist of indicators for spatial sense and 3-D vocabulary

Creativity Skills:

Collaboration

Communication

Opportunities for unique problem solving

Strategic planning

Visualization

Overview:

Children will have a chance to work in pairs as they plan and construct a house using shape blocks. This activity encourages collaborative planning and problem solving and provides opportunities to practice using shape words.

Activity Steps:

1. In advance, create a checklist to determine how well children demonstrate the use of 3-D shape words and development of spatial sense. Build the checklist around the types of 3-D shapes that the children will use in their construction projects. Indicators for development of spatial sense include the ability to manipulate shapes to create a building. Positional words can also be a part of your checklist. See the example that follows, and adapt it as needed.

Example Spatial Visualization Checklist

Position Words		3-D Shape	Notes on Spatial Visualization
_____ above	_____ side	Cylinder	_____ Does the child attempt to slide, turn, and flip items?
_____ below	_____ beside		
_____ up	_____ through		_____ How fluently does the child manipulate the shapes in building?
_____ down	_____ on		
_____ top	_____ over	Cube	
_____ bottom	_____ under		
_____ right	_____ inside		
_____ left	_____ outside		

2. In a whole-group setting, display a variety of 3-D shape blocks. Ask each child to choose one block and tell the group one thing about the shape of the block. Take the time to reinforce 3-D vocabulary—*cube, prism, cylinder, pyramid, sphere,* and *cone*—and other shape words.

3. Explain that the children will be working in pairs to construct a house with the shape blocks.

4. Give each pair a clipboard and pencil, and ask them to work on drawing a plan before they start constructing with the blocks.

5. Throughout the planning and building process, document the children's ability to use shape words and work together collaboratively.

6. Give each pair a variety of shape blocks, and ask them to build their structure. It is best to include a wide variety and a large number of blocks to support building complex structures. Provide a minimum of twenty blocks per pair. Most 3-D geometric block kits include cubes, cylinders, spheres, cones, triangular prisms, and pyramid shapes.

7. Invite the children to use as many of the blocks as they can in their structures. Reassure them that they can take apart their buildings and rebuild as many times as needed to create a stable structure. After each pair has completed a house structure, ask the children questions from the checklist about the shapes they used and the differences and similarities among the shapes. Encourage conversation about why the children used certain blocks to construct their houses.

8. Take photographs of the children with their completed structures. In addition to documentation for portfolios, these photos can be used in future lessons when you ask children to build new structures based on their experiences during this lesson.

Documentation:

Take anecdotal notes on the children's abilities to collaborate, plan, strategize, and solve problems. Fill out a checklist for each pair, indicating the children's ability to use language related to 3-D shapes and demonstrate spatial sense. Save the photos of the children's structures for inclusion in their portfolios.

Extension Lessons:

Children working in pairs can turn this into a building game by setting up a space where their view of the other child is blocked by a table divider or something similar. One child will be the caller and will be responsible for telling the other child which blocks to place and where to place them. The other child will be responsible for listening and attempting to build the same structure as the caller. The pair can remove the table divider at the end and compare their buildings. This experience will require them to use math language and description in order to communicate actions and intent.

You can also promote group building experiences. Children can take turns placing blocks to create structures together. Ask the children to describe the blocks they are using and the placement in relation to the other blocks in the structure. In this way, you can reinforce children's understanding of math words such as *cube, cylinder, near,* and *beside.*

Mapping the School

Topic: Mapping as a way to understand spatial relationships and use position words

Objectives:

Children will create maps of the school or classroom.

Children will use a variety of position words as they explore, plan, and draw their maps.

Materials:

Clipboard

Sketch paper

Pencils

Large drawing paper

Colored pencils

Fine-tipped markers

Teacher-created checklist of indicators for spatial relationships and position words

Creativity Skills:

Collaboration

Communication

Exploration

Problem solving

Documentation

Visualization

Overview:

Children will work individually during this lesson. This activity gives them opportunities to develop their spatial sense and collaborate to use position words to describe features they want to include on their maps.

Activity Steps:

1. In advance, create a checklist of indicators for development of spatial orientation skills. See the example that follows, and adapt it as needed.

Example Spatial Orientation Checklist

Position Words		Notes on Spatial Orientation
_____ above	_____ side	_____ Does the child attend to the location of an object or point of interest on the map?
_____ below	_____ beside	
_____ up	_____ through	
_____ down	_____ on	_____ How does the child attend to the relationship between objects or points of interest (such as distance between points)?
_____ top	_____ over	
_____ bottom	_____ under	
_____ right	_____ inside	_____ To what extent do connections exist between the environment and the child's map?
_____ left	_____ outside	

2. Talk with the children about maps, and ask if they have ever seen or used a map before. Some questions to consider: How are maps used? What do maps help us with? What is included on a map?

3. Show the children a sample map, and point out how it shows locations of interest and features important places. Model using position words—*next to, beside, above, below, under, over, top, bottom, near,* and *far*—to describe the relationship between different features on the map. Explain that each child will develop a map of the school or classroom. They will need to think about which points of interest or locations they will include on their maps.

4. Provide each child with a pencil, clipboard, and sketch paper. Invite the children to use the clipboards and sketch paper to document

their school or classroom as they walk around exploring. They can create draft maps and note important places on their sketches. Be sure to emphasize that each child is drawing her own map and will be able to refine her sketched map once she is back in the classroom for the second part of the lesson.

5. Once the children are back in the classroom, ask them to transfer their sketched maps onto large pieces of drawing paper using colored pencils and fine-tipped markers, refining their sketches on the larger paper.

6. Throughout this process, use your checklist to document how well the children pay attention to locations and use position words.

Documentation:

Take anecdotal notes on the children's ability to collaborate, solve problems, and visualize. Fill out a checklist for each child, noting the child's ability to identify spatial relationships and use position words. Save the maps children create to include in their portfolios.

Extension Lesson:

Send home a detailed explanation about this lesson and request that the children make maps at home of a room or the entire home with adult assistance. Explain what the children can learn by mapping their home environment. You can help the parent or caregiver visualize the project by sending home the sketches children made at school. Be sure to give parents and caregivers enough notice and time to work with their children on the project.

Mapping Our Walk

Topic: Spatial relationships and language and position words

Objectives:

Children will create a map of a simple neighborhood route.

Children will use a variety of position words as they explore, plan, and draw their maps.

Materials:

Clipboard

Sketch paper

Pencils

Teacher-created checklist of indicators for spatial relationships and position words, from the Mapping the School lesson

Overview:

This activity is designed to build on the Mapping the School lesson. Children can revisit the use of maps and practice mapping again during an outdoor experience.

Creativity Skills:

Collaboration

Communication

Documentation

Exploration

Problem solving

Visualization

Activity Steps:

1. Ask the children what they remember from their last mapping experience. It may help if you bring out some examples of those maps for the children to look at. As a refresher, point out how the map shows important places and locations of interest.

2. Explain that today the class will take a walk around the block or neighborhood where the school is located. Encourage the children to think about creating a map to help explain to their parents or caregivers where they went during their walk.

3. Ask the children to use their clipboards, sketch paper, and pencils to document their walk. Stop frequently to give the children time to sketch important features. When you stop, ask the children guiding questions: What do you see? Do you notice any important features that you want to draw on your maps?

4. When you return to the classroom, ask each child to share something from his map that was an important feature on the walk. Discuss some of the differences in the children's map features, encouraging the use of position words.

5. Throughout this process, use your checklist to document how well the children pay attention to location features and use position words.

Documentation:

Take anecdotal notes on the children's ability to collaborate, solve problems, and visualize. Fill out a checklist for the whole group, noting as well as you can when individual children demonstrate knowledge of spatial relationships and use position words accurately. Allow the children to take their maps home and bring them back for inclusion in their portfolios.

Extension Lessons:

Send the children's walking maps home and encourage parents and caregivers to talk with their children about what they saw and did on their walk. Ask families to use the child's map to guide the conversation.

During group time, you can play a location word game. Going around the group, ask each child to name someone she is sitting beside, near, to the right of, to the left of, in front of, or behind.

Children's Books

Hoban, Tana. 1996. *Shapes, Shapes, Shapes.* New York: Greenwillow Books.
Children will enjoy searching the beautiful photographs for various shapes.

MacDonald, Suse. 2009. *Shape by Shape.* New York: Little Simon.
This is a beautiful book with brightly colored, die-cut pages. With the turn of each page, familiar shapes come together to feature a familiar creature.

Thong, Roseanne. *Round Is a Mooncake: A Book of Shapes.* San Francisco: Chronicle.
Vibrant artwork featuring traditional Chinese colors and patterns invites readers to explore the shapes found among Chinese cultural objects.

5
Measurement

Making comparisons between objects is a regular activity for preschoolers. The close scrutiny that surrounds the splitting of a cookie between friends demonstrates that very young children are capable of making comparisons. Comparison is the first step in developing an understanding of measurement. During the preschool years, children should have regular opportunities to use their senses to make comparisons and use standard and nonstandard tools to support their measurement activities.

In informal experiences and planned lessons, we use measurement to observe and record information about the length, height, weight, or even depth of objects and people. Preschoolers will benefit from opportunities to explore measurement traits using nonstandard measurement tools before using standard tools such as rulers and scales. Early experiences using nonstandard measurement tools—such as a piece of string to measure the height of growing plants—promote opportunities to explore and compare various objects using standard measuring tools. As children gain familiarity and comfort with nonstandard measurement and comparison, you can introduce standard measurement tools to extend their understanding.

As you plan activities involving measurement, consider the relevant guidance and standards provided by the NCTM:

Measurement

Understand measurable attributes of objects and the units, systems, and processes of measurement

In pre-K through grade 2 all students should—

- recognize the attributes of length, volume, weight, area, and time;

- compare and order objects according to these attributes;

- understand how to measure using nonstandard and standard units;

- select an appropriate unit and tool for the attribute being measured.

Apply appropriate techniques, tools, and formulas to determine measurements

In pre-K through grade 2 all students should—

- measure with multiple copies of units of the same size, such as paper clips laid end to end;

- use repetition of a single unit to measure something larger than the unit, for instance, measure the length of a room with a single meterstick;

- use tools to measure;

- develop common referents for measures to make comparisons and estimates.

Source: National Council of Teachers of Mathematics. 2000. Principles and Standards for School Mathematics. Reston, VA: NCTM. Reproduced with permission.

The Processes of Measurement

The following types of explorations can help children develop their measurement skills:

- **Identifying the attribute**—Children gain awareness of the physical attributes of objects in order to identify measurement possibilities.

- **Using direct comparison**—Children look for similarities and differences between two or more objects. Examples of direct comparison include placing two or more objects side by side for exploration. Children might place two toy cars next to each other to explore which is bigger, stand back to back to explore height, or place a thick marker next to a thin marker to explore which marker will make thicker lines.

- **Using indirect comparison**—Children find ways to check for similarities and differences between objects when they cannot be placed directly together. Examples of indirect comparison experiences can be drawn from the children's everyday lives. Children can compare two trees on the playground to find out which has a larger tree trunk by using a piece of string to measure the circumference of the base of each tree.

- **Measuring with nonstandard tools**—Nonstandard measurement involves the use of ordinary objects to establish measurement data. A child might use a crayon as a unit of measurement. Children can line up crayons end to end to measure the length of classroom toys. Each crayon would be considered a unit, so a toy fire truck might be 6 units long.

Vignette for Understanding: Documentation and Measurement

A small group of students is gathered around a table with samples of student work from a long-term science investigation on plants. The group is assisting Mrs. Knight as she plans out a documentation panel of the class's project work. Mrs. Knight asks

Griffin and Sara to figure out how many photographs they can fit on the top half of the panel. She encourages Griffin to measure with his string to come up with the total number. Griffin has lengths of string that are equal to the size of the photos they will post to the board. He carefully lays out a piece of string starting from the top left corner. As he works his way across, Sara is adding tally marks to her paper each time Griffin adds another string. The last full piece of string to fit across the board brings the pair's total to nine. Sara and Griffin share the number with Mrs. Knight, and she asks them to select the nine photographs that will be used in the display.

Reflection

Griffin and Sara were able to use nonstandard measurement to determine the ideal number of objects for their task. Mrs. Knight helped to scaffold the process by ensuring that the children had supportive materials—string, paper, and pencils—to successfully and independently measure length. Placing children in pairs to work during measurement experiences can also serve as a source of support as children face complex tasks. Early learning experiences in measurement should allow for a close examination of the object, comparison of attributes, and opportunities for nonstandard measurement.

Planning Tips for Integrating Measurement

Measurement can involve many different types of materials, and it is important to introduce children to measurement materials in an open-ended, exploratory manner. A math manipulative center is a good location for measurement materials—children can freely explore and experiment so that they become familiar with these materials during play. When you introduce standard measurement material—scales, measuring cups and spoons, and rulers—you can help children become comfortable using these tools by encouraging their inquiry and scaffolding their explorations. Be sure to connect the use of measurement tools to experiences that are personally meaningful to the child, such as the use of measuring cups and spoons to make a favorite snack or drink.

Questions for Inquiry and Exploration

You can use the following types of questions to encourage guided-inquiry explorations in measurement:

- How tall is your tower?

- Which of these is longer? How do you know that?

- What can I do to find out which of these is heavier?

- How many counters do you think it will take to measure your block path?

- Which of these is bigger or smaller, or heaviest or lightest? Why do you think that?

- We need 2 cups of flour. Which of these helps us measure 2 cups?

Lesson Ideas

Big and Little Nature Hunt

Topic: Comparing length

Objective:

Children will identify and compare the length of nature items.

Materials:

Clipboard

Paper

Pencils

Colored pencils, crayons, markers, or watercolor paints

Overview:

In this introductory lesson, children will make observations related to the size of natural objects and document their observations with paper and pencils. Depending on the resources available outside your school building, you might ask the children to look for objects in the schoolyard, or you might take the children on a walk to collect items from nature.

Activity Steps:

1. Tell the children they will explore the area outside the classroom and look for big and little versions of objects. A child might collect a big rock and a little one or a big leaf and a little one.

2. Provide each child with a pencil, clipboard, and sketch paper. Ask the children to document the size of their objects on their papers. Children can draw by hand or trace objects if they prefer.

3. Talk with the children about their findings, and encourage them to find additional objects to compare. Ask questions such as the following: How do you know that is the bigger leaf? Why do you think this leaf is little? These types of guided-inquiry questions can support their thinking and provide opportunities for you to gauge their understandings.

4. When children return to the classroom, explain that they can use colored pencils, crayons, markers, or watercolor paints to continue illustrating their big and little items from nature.

Documentation:

Take anecdotal notes on the children's abilities to explore the size of objects. The children's illustrations comparing sizes could go in their portfolios.

Extension Lesson:

Explore other comparisons such as wide and narrow and long and short.

Me-Size Towers

Topic: Comparing length

Objective:

Children will build block towers that reach their height.

Materials:

Building blocks in a variety of sizes

Mirror

Digital camera (optional)

Creativity Skills:

Exploration

Problem solving

Visualization

Overview:

Children will work to build towers as tall as they are. This lesson works best if children work in pairs or small groups so they have adequate access to needed materials and help from peers.

Activity Steps:

1. Start with a whole-group discussion about estimating height. Begin by asking children if they have ever made a tower as tall as themselves. Ask how many blocks they think it will take to make a teacher-size tower. Use children as examples of tower height: "How about a Kyra-size tower or one as tall as Deon?"

2. Divide the children into pairs or small groups, and ask them to find enough space to begin working on their towers.

3. Encourage the children to think about their tower's base size, so it will support other blocks as children add to the tower.

4. Periodically ask the children to count the number of blocks they have used so far and to estimate how many more they will need.

Have the builders stand next to their tower while you hold up a mirror to show them how close they are to creating a tower as tall as they are.

5. After each tower is complete, you can take a photograph of the children standing next to it, if desired.

Documentation:

Take anecdotal notes on the children's abilities to estimate the relative height of their towers. You can also take photographs of the builders with their completed towers.

Extension Lesson:

Invite the children to use the blocks to build towers that are smaller than their bodies or larger than their bodies.

Comparing Nonstandard Measurements

Topic: Estimating the length of objects using nonstandard measurement

Objectives:

Children will use nonstandard measurement to estimate the length of objects.

Children will compare the results of the nonstandard measurement of an object.

Materials:

Variety of nonstandard measurement tools including cubes, colored counters, dominoes, and craft sticks

Five to seven classroom items of various sizes to be measured

Math journals

Pencils

Creativity Skills:

Exploration

Documentation

Visualization

Overview:

Children will work in pairs to measure a variety of items using nonstandard measurement tools. Each pair will use different tools. After completing their measurements, the children will discuss the differences in their results.

Activity Steps:

1. In advance, place the various-sized classroom items around the classroom so the children will have enough space to work.

2. In a whole-group setting, introduce the children to the topic of nonstandard measurement by using colored counters to measure the size of their feet. You can ask the following types of questions during the process: How many counters do you think it will take to measure your feet? If John's foot was eleven counters long, how many do you think it will take to measure yours? Why?

3. Once the children understand the process of measuring with nonstandard items, group children in pairs. Be sure to give each pair a different measurement tool. Invite the children to circulate around the room and measure the different classroom items you have selected.

4. Encourage the children to use their math journals to document the number of counters (or other tools) they use to measure each item.

5. Once the children have completed their work, invite them back to the whole group to share their results. Have a discussion about how many of the different kinds of counters it took to measure each item. You might ask the following types of questions: Did we use more cubes or more craft sticks to measure the book? Why did it take fewer craft sticks? Be sure to display the measurement tools and the items during your discussion so that children have an immediate visual representation.

Documentation:

Take anecdotal notes on the children's ability to measure using nonstandard tools and to compare the results. Review students' notes in their math journals.

Extension Lesson:

Introduce more student choice into this activity once children gain experience with the process of nonstandard measurement. Invite children to choose their measurement tools and the items to be measured. Documentation in their math journals will be important to keep track of their explorations.

Equal Weights?

Topic: Estimating the weight of small objects

Objectives:

Children will estimate the similarity or difference in the weight of classroom items.

Children will use a balance scale to explore their estimations.

Materials:

Balance scale

Small classroom items for measurement

Student math journals

Creativity Skills:

Exploration

Problem solving

Visualization

Overview:

This activity allows children to compare different items and estimate their relative weights. Then they can confirm their predictions using a balance scale. This practice will help them think critically and refine their abilities to estimate weight.

Activity Steps:

1. In a whole-group setting, introduce the balance scale and invite the children to see a demonstration of the scale. Discuss how the scale shows us the weight of one item relative to another. Using two identical objects, ask the children if they think they will weigh the same or if one will weigh more. Following their responses, ask why so that they can clarify their thinking.

2. Using two different objects, ask the children for estimations, and use the scale to check children's predictions.

3. Tell the children that you will put the balance scale in the math center, and they can continue estimating the relative weight of different items and then weighing them on the scale.

4. Explain to the children that they can draw pictures of the items in their math journals. You can create or help the children create a simple table on the page with two headings: "Heavier" and "Lighter." Children can draw pictures of or write the names of the objects they weigh under the appropriate heading. If the objects weighed are the same weight, ask the children to brainstorm ways of representing items of equal weight in their journal.

5. While children use the scale in the math center, ask them questions about their estimations and their results to help them continue thinking critically and refining their understandings.

Documentation:

Take anecdotal notes on the children's abilities to measure weight using standard tools and to compare and discuss the results. Review the drawings in the students' math journals as a primary source of documentation.

Extension Lesson:

You can introduce more student choice once they gain experience with the process of standard measurement. Invite children to choose their measurement tools—rulers, measuring cups and spoons, or digital or balance scales—and the items to be measured or weighed. Ask them to document their investigations in their math journals.

Measuring: Cornstarch Fingerpaint

Topic: Learning about the tools used for measuring during cooking—measuring cups and measuring spoons

Objective:

The children will help measure the liquid and dry ingredients to create different colors of cornstarch fingerpaints.

Materials:

Measuring cups and spoons

Large bowl

Two to four small bowls

Spoon for stirring

½ cup cornstarch

2 cups water

Different colors of liquid food coloring

Large sheets of coated paper

Overview:

Children will measure and mix fingerpaint and then paint with the mixture. This lesson will work best if children work alongside you in small groups of three or four.

Activity Steps:

1. In a small-group setting, invite the children to look at the measuring cups and spoons. Ask them questions about the different sizes of tools. What do they notice as they pass the materials around? Which cup or spoon is the biggest? Which is the smallest? Talk to them about how they will use those tools to measure ingredients to make fingerpaint.

2. Work alongside the children so they can measure and mix the cornstarch and water for the fingerpaint base.

3. Divide the noncolored mixture into at least two bowls, and have the children choose and add food coloring to create different paint colors in each bowl.

4. Provide coated paper for children to use as they explore fingerpainting.

Documentation:

Take anecdotal notes on the children's abilities to measure using the measurement tools, and compare and discuss the various sizes of tools.

Extension Lessons:

You can gradually introduce more-complex cooking activities. In each lesson, be sure to invite children to discuss what they notice about the sizes of the measurement tools. Using the appropriate language—*cup, half cup, teaspoon,* and *tablespoon*—will help extend their understanding of measurement.

After the children mix up primary colors of paint, you can introduce mixing primary colors to make secondary colors. The children can experiment with this process by mixing the paint on their papers or by combining food coloring in the bowls of paint.

Time Books

Topic: Describing the time and sequence of the day as it applies to the child's daily schedule

Objective:

The children will use appropriate vocabulary when describing the sequence of time—*day, morning, afternoon,* and *evening.*

Materials:

Various colors of 8½" x 11" construction paper

Hole punch

String or yarn

Markers, pencils, and crayons

Creativity Skills:

Collaboration

Communication

Documentation

Overview:

Children will think about their daily activities and the sequence of their day. They will illustrate major activities on paper and put the activities in order of time of the day in a book. This activity works best in small groups so that you can carefully guide children through the process of creating their books.

Activity Steps:

1. In advance, cut the construction paper in half so that you have sheets about 8½" x 5½". Use a hole punch to make two holes on the left side of each sheet in a landscape layout to give children maximum space to draw. Provide each child with five to ten sheets and two pieces of yarn or string about 8 inches long. Tell the children they will be creating books about their daily activities, and they will tie their pages together after they complete their books.

2. In each small group, ask the children what they do in the morning before coming to school. You might talk about eating breakfast, getting dressed, and walking or traveling to school. Ask the children to think carefully about what they do in the morning, afternoon, and evening. Children can draw or write about their activities on the construction paper pages. Inviting the children to put one activity on each page will support their thinking about the sequencing of activities.

3. Help the children think about the order of their activities and put the pages in the order they describe. If they begin to place activities out of order, ask targeted questions: Do you eat breakfast before or after lunch? Do you take naps at school before or after lunch? Reinforce the terminology of *day, morning, afternoon,* and *evening*.

4. When the children have completed their pages, add a cover page for each book with a title written on it. You or the child can write "Shonda's Day," for example, and then the child can illustrate the cover. Encourage the children to pull string through the punched holes, and assist them in tying the string as needed.

Documentation:

Take anecdotal notes on the children's ability to understand time sequences and use the targeted vocabulary. Consider saving the students' day books for their portfolios.

Extension Lesson:

You can send the time books home along with blank pages for children to describe their mornings and evenings in more detail or to add their weekend schedules. With assistance from family members, children can write about or illustrate the additional activities on the new pages.

Countdown Chain

Topic: Understanding the duration of a week

Objective:

The children will count the days of a week or weeks to a desired event.

Materials:

2" x 8" strips of construction paper, making groups of seven in the same color

Tape

> **Creativity Skill:**
>
> Visualization

Overview:

Children will create a chain made of paper links that will help them count down the number of days until a specific event occurs. The chain can be used to reinforce the idea of seven days in each week.

Activity Steps:

1. In advance, prepare the construction paper loops in the appropriate colors. Each color used can correspond to a particular day of the week. However, if the event is more than a week away, then seven loops could be in one color and the next seven loops could be in a different color.

2. Have the children sit together to look at a traditional calendar with a particular event noted on the calendar. Working from today, count the number of days until the arrival of the scheduled event.

3. Discuss the days of the week with the children. As you talk about the days of the week, pass out the strips of colored paper. One at a time, invite the children to bring their strips forward and add them to the chain, taping each one into a loop shape linked through the previous loop. Once the chain has the desired number of days represented, talk with the children about how the class will remove one link each day to help mark the time until the scheduled event.

4. As a child removes a link each day, have all of the children perform a countdown with you.

Documentation:

Take anecdotal notes on the children's abilities to restate the days of the week and count toward the scheduled event.

Extension Lesson:

Parents and guardians can re-create this activity at home to reinforce their child's understanding of the number of days in a week. Sending home a description of the assignment with strips of paper will work to encourage parents to count down to an important family event.

Children's Books

Leedy, Loreen. 1997. *Measuring Penny*. New York: Henry Holt.
   This book invites you to follow along with Lisa and her dog Penny as they use standard and nonstandard measurement to measure household items.

Lionni, Leo. 1995. *Inch by Inch*. New York: HarperCollins.
   This is a classic read that asks children to follow along as an inchworm measures his world.

Ward, Cindy. 1997. *Cookie's Week*. New York: Puffin.
   Follow along with Cookie the cat as she has new adventures every day of the week.

6
Data Collection and Statistics

Young children are naturally curious and spend a large portion of their day asking questions in search of answers. We can build upon their natural tendency to ask questions by carefully listening and responding to their questions. We can help them to further their thinking by encouraging them to ask questions, collect answers, and then talk about what they learned. A natural entry point for collecting and analyzing data is through sorting and counting experiences. Early childhood teachers can strategically expand classroom sorting and counting experiences to include more formal skills, such as collecting specific data and identifying patterns. Young children can also participate in responding to simple two-question surveys and posing survey questions to others so they can collect response data.

Children will need initial support and guidance in creating and responding to simple surveys. Children will often want to place more than one vote—"I'd like to walk to the park and to the fire station"—or they may be upset when the choice they voted for is not part of the majority. In these instances, be patient with the children and talk about why each person gets to place only one vote. Reassure them that every vote is important. As children gain more experience with personally meaningful surveys or data collection experiences, those experiences will promote a deeper understanding of the processes of both data collection and analysis.

As you plan activities that allow children to collect data and think about the results, consider the relevant guidance and standards provided by NCTM:

Data Analysis and Probability

Formulate questions that can be addressed with data, and collect, organize, and display relevant data to answer them

In pre-K through grade 2 all students should—

- pose questions and gather data about themselves and their surroundings;

- sort and classify objects according to their attributes and organize data about the objects;

- represent data using concrete objects, pictures, and graphs.

Select and use appropriate statistical methods to analyze data

In pre-K through grade 2 all students should—

- describe parts of the data and the set of data as a whole to determine what the data show.

Develop and evaluate inferences and predictions that are based on data

In pre-K through grade 2 all students should—

- discuss events related to students' experiences as likely or unlikely.

Source: National Council of Teachers of Mathematics. 2000. *Principles and Standards for School Mathematics.* Reston, VA: NCTM. Reproduced with permission.

One way to introduce the process of data collection is to pose a simple yes-or-no question to the children at circle time. Counting the children's responses and sharing the results is an important step in understanding why we collect data. Children should have many experiences with data collection and organization related to questions of personal interest to them.

- What should we name the class pet?

- Do you like chocolate or vanilla better?

- Should we go on a walk or play an outside game?

Once children pose or respond to a question, early childhood teachers can help children organize and display their data in a format they can understand. The process of understanding data organization can actually begin with either informal or formal sorting experiences. The process of sorting encourages children to think about the way objects are similar or different.

Vignette for Understanding: Data Collection

It's an exciting day in the four-year-old classroom. A new fish has joined the class's fish tank. The children are working with their teacher, Becca, to choose a name for their new fish. Three names have been offered—Nemo, Red Guy, and Magic. Becca has posted a large sheet of paper at the front of the room with each of the three names in a column. She has also given each child a sticky note and directed them to put their sticky note under the name they want to vote for. Children walk to the front of the room one by one and carefully consider their selections. There's much excitement! It looks like Magic will be the new name, as seven out of the ten children have voted for it. Becca asks the class to count along. They count two votes for Nemo, one vote for Red Guy, and seven votes for Magic. "Magic it is. Magic got more votes than the other names," announces Becca. "Let's be sure to welcome Magic into our classroom."

Reflection

Becca took advantage of a natural opportunity to encourage children to collect data and use that data to draw a conclusion. The voting process allowed the children to clearly see how each vote was counted in the final decision and was presented in a way that the children could understand.

Graphing

Graphing provides children with opportunities to display and share information that they have collected. When children are able to create and share a graph about a question or topic that interests them, they see how mathematics can be communicated to others in a personally meaningful way. In early childhood classrooms, graphing should take place in three stages:

- **Stage 1**—Children will place real objects on a graphing mat or in a pocket chart.

- **Stage 2**—Teachers will introduce pictorial graphs. Children will place pictures that represent the real objects on a graph.

- **Stage 3**—Teachers will introduce symbolic graphs. In this advanced stage, children use words, numbers, or symbols to represent the data collected.

In the classroom vignette with Becca and Magic, the class used a symbolic graph. Each child's vote was represented by a sticky note placed in the desired column. By counting the sticky notes for each of the proposed names aloud with the children, Becca supported the children's understanding that each vote would be added to the others to create the outcome. As children build their experience with graphing, it is helpful to encourage them to count the objects, numbers, or words represented on the graph aloud and talk together about what the number means.

Planning Tips for Integrating Data Collection and Statistics

Collecting information to answer questions of interest to children can be a regular and consistent part of your mathematics teaching. You can use descriptive language—*more*, *fewer*, or *the same*—to help describe the data displays children create in order to support their analysis of the collected data. Data should be personally meaningful to the children so they can see direct connections from data and graphs to their everyday experiences.

Questions for Inquiry and Exploration

- What question could you ask to find that out?

- We can take a vote. What are the two ideas we are voting on?

- What do you want to find out?

- How can you show a friend what you are thinking?

Lesson Ideas

Our Favorite Color

Topic: Collect information to answer questions of interest

Objectives:

Children will participate in the collection of data about class members' favorite colors.

Children will use descriptive language to compare data by identifying which is *more*, *fewer*, or *the same* in the resulting graph.

Materials:

Sticky notes in the colors yellow, orange, red, green, blue, and purple

Large piece of chart paper

Marker

Creativity Skills:

Documentation

Exploration

Visualization

Overview:

In this introductory lesson, each child will choose the color he likes best and tape it to the corresponding column on the graph.

Activity Steps:

1. In advance, divide the chart paper into six columns with a marker. Label the columns yellow, orange, red, green, blue, and purple. Post the chart paper on a wall or attach it to a bulletin board. Place the sticky notes on a table near the paper.

2. Explain to the children that they will be creating a graph so that the class will be able to see what the children's overall favorite colors are.

3. Let the children take turns walking to the color graph and placing one of the colored sticky notes in the corresponding favorite color column, starting at the bottom. Show the children how to place their note directly above the previous one in a column to create a bar graph.

4. Once each child has placed a sticky note on the graph, count the number in each column along with the children.

5. Ask questions such as the following: Which has more? How do you know that? To summarize the findings, you could ask: Which is the most favorite color? Which color do we like the least?

6. Post the graph in the classroom, so the children can refer to it for future graphing experiences.

Documentation:

Take anecdotal notes on the children's abilities to sort colors and place their selections on the color graph. Post the completed color graph as both a reminder and a resource for the children.

Extension Lesson:

Ask children to graph with other representational objects. For example, you could make a weather graph so the children can predict the day's weather. Make cutouts of suns, clouds, and raindrops and label the graph with a column for each. At the end of the day, review the graph and see how accurate the children's predictions were.

Colors-of-Nature Graph

Topic: Sort and compare natural objects by similarities and differences in color

Objectives:

Children will collect and sort natural objects by color.

Children will sort natural objects in columns on a color graph.

Children will use descriptive language to compare data by identifying which is *more*, *fewer*, or *the same* in the object graphs.

Materials:

Paper bags

Large piece of chart paper

Digital camera (optional)

Creativity Skills:

Documentation

Exploration

Visualization

Overview:

You and the children will go on a walk outside, collecting items from nature. Back in the classroom, the children will sort their collected items by color.

Activity Steps:

1. In advance, ask children what colors they have seen in nature. You might ask what colors of flowers or rocks they have seen before.

2. With a marker, draw six to eight columns on the chart paper. Label columns with the colors the children have volunteered during the discussion. Leave a few columns blank, and label them later.

3. Invite the children to join you on a nature walk to collect small items of different colors. Give each child a paper bag for collecting the items. You can encourage children to discuss the colors they are seeing during the walk.

4. Once you are all back in the classroom, provide space for the children to sort their items by color. Invite the children to help name all of the colors they see.

5. Place the color graph on the floor, adding new color labels for the blank columns as needed. Once the children are finished sorting, invite each child to place one chosen object on the graph on the corresponding color.

6. After each child has placed an item, you can ask what the children notice about the graph: Which color has the most items? Which has the fewest number of items?

7. You can use the leftover nature items in the math center for the children to continue to sort.

Documentation:

Take anecdotal notes on the children's ability to sort objects by color and place them on the color graph. Use the completed color graph as evidence of the children's ability to understand colors. You can photograph it for future reference if you like.

Extension Lesson:

This activity can support science-related lessons during each season so the children can explore the different colors in nature at different times of the year. Taking photographs of the completed graphs will allow them the opportunity to compare and contrast the colors of the seasons.

The Big Sort

Topic: Sort and compare objects by similarities and differences

Objectives:

Children will sort objects by an identified attribute.

Children will document their sorting attribute in their math journal.

Materials:

Math journals

Pencils, markers, crayons, and colored pencils

Classroom items of various sizes and colors— colored pompoms, counting bears, Unifix cubes, small animal figures, or blocks

Containers of various sizes for sorting

Creativity Skills:

Collaboration

Communication

Documentation

Exploration

Visualization

Overview:

Children will have opportunities to brainstorm ways to sort varied classroom items and then actually sort them by attributes.

Activity Steps:

1. Place the mix of classroom items on a table along with a variety of containers for sorting. Invite children to join you at the table and bring their math journals. Children can work individually or alongside others in a small group.

2. Looking at the mix of objects, ask the children how they might sort the items so that they aren't all mixed up. Listen to children's ideas or watch their actions and prompt them to think about why their approach would work. Encourage them by saying, "That's a great idea. Can you think of another way we could sort these objects?" You might prompt

Creative Investigations in Early Math

them by asking what they notice about the objects, and what makes the objects the same or different.

3.   Once the children have thought through a few different sorting attributes, encourage them to begin to sort the objects into different containers.

4.   After the children are done sorting, ask them to use their math journals to document the sorting attributes they chose. They might color, draw, or trace the objects.

Documentation:

Take anecdotal notes on the children's abilities to collaborate, solve problems, and visualize. Review students' math journals to assess their learning.

Extension Lesson:

Children should have many different sorting experiences with a variety of objects including natural items. By changing up the groupings of objects, you can help the children understand similarities and differences. For example, if you notice that a child always sorts by color, provide that child with a collection of various objects of the same color. This will push children's thinking in new directions as they explore differences in size, material type, or ways objects can be used.

Guess What I'm Thinking

Topic: Sort and compare objects by similarities and differences

Objective:

Children will sort and identify objects by chosen attributes.

Materials:

Classroom items of various sizes and colors— colored pompoms, counting bears, Unifix cubes, small animal figures, or blocks

Table divider

Creativity Skills:

Collaboration

Communication

Exploration

Problem solving

Visualization

Overview:

Children will work in pairs to play a sorting game. With a divider between the two children, one will sort a mix of items, and then one will guess what attribute the sorter used.

Activity Steps:

1. Divide children into pairs and give each duo a pile of mixed items. Place the table divider between the two children.

2. Explain that the children will alternate being either the sorter or the guesser. The sorter gets to sort the items by a chosen attribute, such as color or size. Once the sorting is finished, the guesser will get to peek around the table divider and guess the attribute that the sorter used to place the items into groups.

3. Let the children play the game. With each turn, encourage the children to be creative with their chosen attribute to increase the complexity of the game.

4. After the guessing is done, ask the sorter to explain her thinking to the guesser. If prompting is needed, you might ask what is the same among the groups.

Documentation:

Take anecdotal notes on the children's ability to collaborate, solve problems, and visualize.

Extension Lesson:

As children gain experience with sorting, encourage them to collect their own objects to sort. This will extend the possibilities for sorting and encourage them to plan and think in creative ways.

Let's Take a Vote

Topic: Integrated social studies and math lesson

Objectives:

Children will participate in a group voting experience.

Children will collect information to answer a question of interest.

Children will use descriptive language to compare data by identifying which is *more, fewer,* or *the same* in the graph.

Materials:

Large chart paper

Fine-tipped markers

Sticky notes in a variety of colors

Overview:

Children will think of a question for voting that involves a few possible answers. Then the children will cast votes to create a simple graph.

Creativity Skills:

Collaboration

Communication

Documentation

Exploration

Problem solving

Activity Steps:

1. Talk with the children about graphs and ask if they have ever seen one before. Here are some questions to consider: How are graphs used? When do we use graphs? What can we learn from a graph? Show the children a sample graph and discuss what the meaning of each column tells us. It is helpful if your sample graph is a simple one involving the children. For example, you can create a graph of the number of children age four and age five with their names in the corresponding columns to use as an example.

2. Ask the class to think of a question of interest that they would like to vote on. The name of a new class fish and the destination of a class walk are possibilities for exploration.

3. Decide on the choices for voting, and then draw columns on the chart paper for the different votes that are possible.

4. Explain that each child will get to cast one vote with a colored sticky note or by writing his name in his chosen column. Invite the children to cast their votes one by one.

5. Encourage the class to count out the end result of the voting process using the mathematics language of *more*, *fewer*, or *the same*.

Documentation:

Take anecdotal notes on the children's abilities to collaborate, solve problems, and take turns. Use the class graph as evidence of the children's learning.

Extension Lesson:

This lesson can be turned into a regular experience in your classroom by conducting a survey of the day. You can pose a simple question each day to your students and have them move their name tag under their chosen response. Questions should be personal to the children and offer just two choices: Should we take the balls or the bubbles out to the playground? Should we have grape or apple juice at snack time? After the voting is complete, have the children tally the results. Let all children know the results. More choices can be added to the survey questions once they demonstrate their understanding of the process.

Children's Books

Harris, Trudy. 2010. *Tally Cat Keeps Track.* Minneapolis, MN: Millbrook Press.
    Follow along on the adventures of Tally McNally, an alley cat who loves to tally.

Murphy, Stuart J. 2005. *Tally O'Malley.* New York: HarperCollins.
    Play along with the book's characters as they play tally games.

7
Patterns and Relationships

Patterning is fundamental to mathematics and serves as the cornerstone of algebraic thinking. Early childhood patterning skills include being able to recognize, extend, create, and copy patterns. Using the core pattern at least three times in a row will help children see the repetition and the pattern more clearly. The simplest pattern to introduce to children—known as an AB pattern—involves two variables. For example, you can line up colored counters in a sequence of red, blue, red, blue, red, blue to make an AB pattern. More complex patterns can include ABC, AABB, or ABCD. Patterning involves the recognition of relationships between objects. Young children can use patterns to predict or explain the relationships between objects. For example, in an AB pattern a child could predict that a blue counter follows a red counter as she extends the pattern.

As you plan activities that will help children understand patterns, consider the relevant guidance and standards provided by NCTM:

Algebra

Understand patterns, relations, and functions

In pre-K through grade 2 all students should—

- sort, classify, and order objects by size, number, and other properties;

- recognize, describe, and extend patterns such as sequences of sounds and shapes or simple numeric patterns and translate from one representation to another;

- analyze how both repeating and growing patterns are generated.

Source: National Council of Teachers of Mathematics. 2000. *Principles and Standards for School Mathematics.* Reston, VA: NCTM. Reproduced with permission.

Vignette for Understanding: Music Patterns

Mrs. Sunday's class is gathered around the circle-time rug selecting instruments to play. Mrs. Sunday is going to challenge the class to line up in an ABC pattern to play their instruments. Children selecting bells are As, children selecting drums are Bs, and children selecting whistles are Cs. Mrs. Sunday encourages the children to remember their letters and think about who they should be standing next to. She asks, "If I'm a B and have a drum, should I have another drum next to me?" A unanimous "no" comes from children helping to direct their classmates into the line. As children are shuffling, Mrs. Sunday keeps repeating, "ABC, bells, drums, and whistles." Once the children have settled into place, she asks if they are ready to test their pattern. "Yes!" they respond. Mrs. Sunday states, "Carver is at the start of the line, so he can start the pattern. Ready. Set. Go." The children play one note on each instrument down their pattern line. After the last note is played, Mrs. Sunday exclaims, "You did it! You did it! A perfect ABC pattern!"

Reflection

Mrs. Sunday's class gives a great example of an integrated math and music content lesson. The task of creating an ABC pattern was an active experience for the children. Mrs. Sunday's questions and reminders served to support student thinking during the activity. A whole-group learning experience also provides opportunities for children to learn from and support their peers.

Planning Tips for Integrating Patterns and Relationships

Although patterning is an important component of early mathematics learning, it is also a feature of other content areas. Patterning opportunities occur across the content areas of science, art, language, music, and movement. Integrating mathematics ideas and language into the patterning experiences in these content areas will help create cross-curricular connections and strengthen children's patterning skills as they seek to understand relationships from a variety of perspectives.

Questions for Inquiry and Exploration

- What do you notice when you look at that picture?

- Do you see any differences between these objects?

- How can you add on to that pattern to keep it growing?

- What comes next? How do you know?

- Do these things go together?

- Are they the same or different?

Lesson Ideas

Recognizing Attributes

Topic: Sort and classify objects according to one or two attributes— color, size, shape, or texture

Objectives:

Children will sort objects by an identified attribute.

Children will document their sorting attribute in their math journal.

Materials:

Pencils, markers, crayons, or colored pencils

Large chart paper

Tape

A mix of classroom items of various sizes and colors—colored pompoms, counting bears, Unifix cubes, small animal figures, or blocks

Containers for sorting

Digital camera (optional)

Creativity Skills:

Collaboration

Communication

Documentation

Exploration

Visualization

Overview:

This lesson builds on previous sorting experiences in chapter 6 by encouraging children's work in the math center. Children can work individually or alongside others in a small group to sort a mixture of items in different ways.

Activity Steps:

1. In advance, title the chart paper "How I Sorted," and divide the area below into two columns. Label the left-hand column for the children's names and the right-hand column for their sorting criteria. Tape the chart paper to the wall.

2. Place the mix of items in the math center. Invite children to go there during center time and look for different attributes they can use to sort the items—color, size, shape, or texture.

3. Observe as the children discover ways to sort the mix, and encourage them to document their criteria by coloring, drawing, or tracing objects' selected sorting attributes on the chart paper.

4. Support children in their documentation by helping them spell descriptive words or by taking digital photos of the sorted items for display.

5. After the sorting experience has been in the center for a few days, bring the "How I Sorted" documentation paper to whole-group time to discuss all of the different attributes the children discovered and put to use.

Documentation:

Review the "How I Sorted" documentation paper and digital photos, if taken.

Extension Lesson:

Children can sort again using a variety of media and materials, including natural objects and mathematics manipulatives.

Classmate Patterns

Topic: Sort and classify objects according to one or two attributes—color, size, shape, or texture

Objective:

Children will cooperatively create a pattern with other children in a whole-group setting.

Materials:

Digital camera

Overview:

You will sort children into two groups according to an attribute, and then ask them to line up in a repeating AB pattern. Children will physically experience the repeating pattern.

Creativity Skills:

Collaboration

Communication

Exploration

Visualization

Activity Steps:

1. During whole-group time, remind the children that patterns have repeating elements.

2. Divide the children into two groups based on a selected attribute, such as long hair and short hair, long sleeves and short sleeves, and solid shirts and patterned shirts.

3. Create a simple AB pattern by inviting children to line up according to alternating attributes. "Trina has long hair. Jaxon has short hair. Cassidy has long hair. What comes next? Do I need a child with long or short hair to keep this pattern growing?" Encourage children to call out what comes next and review the pattern when completed.

4. It will be helpful to work through at least two different patterns with the children during the group setting to help them practice and apply their thinking about patterning.

5. Encourage children to think about alternative attributes that they can use to sort themselves and create a pattern.

6. Take a photograph of each completed pattern for display in the math center so the children can revisit the patterns and use them as a reference.

Documentation:

Take anecdotal notes on children's abilities to recognize and apply attribute information to patterns. Photograph the patterns of children standing in lines.

Extension Lesson:

Provide many opportunities for children to use patterns. This activity could become a favorite group-time lesson if children are provided repeated experiences with sorting and patterning. This lesson can be extended by asking children to create emotion patterns—happy face, sad face, happy face, sad face—along with other attribute patterns.

Patterning Trays

Topic: Sort and classify objects according to one or two attributes—color, size, shape, or texture

Objective:

Children will sort objects by a selected attribute.

Materials:

Pattern strips—1" x 8" strips of paper with lines drawn to mark each inch

Individual trays to create a workspace

Small collection of manipulatives:

- Shape patterns—pattern blocks or buttons

- Color patterns—animal counters, color counters, or Unifix cubes

- Size patterns—craft materials, such as pompoms, or animal family counters

Overview:

Children will practice creating patterns using patterns strips and small items.

Activity Steps:

1. Place individual trays with pattern strips and a collection of manipulatives in the math center or on a table where children can access them. Demonstrate for the children how they can use the pattern strips and items to create a pattern. Tell the children that they will get to create their own patterns.

2. Work alongside the children in the beginning to be sure they understand how to create patterns. Begin a simple AB pattern—such as red bear, blue bear, red bear, blue bear, red bear. Ask the children to look for the pattern and think about what comes next.

3. Encourage the children to talk about and explain their thinking. Modeling your description of the pattern can be helpful. "I used a red bear, and then a blue bear, and then a red bear. What color do I need to use next to keep my pattern growing?" As children finish the pattern, ask them to talk about their pattern.

4. Encourage the children to create their own new patterns using the pattern strips.

Documentation:

Review the children's completed pattern strips and take anecdotal notes on their abilities to recognize and apply attribute information.

Extension Lesson:

Give the children opportunities to work with a variety of media and materials in the math center, including natural objects and mathematics manipulatives, to practice creating patterns using the pattern strips. Encourage them to try patterns of increasing complexity.

Patterns in Our World

Topic: Identifying preexisting patterns in the environment

Objective:

Children will work together to seek out and identify patterns in their environment.

Materials:

Digital camera

Overview:

In this lesson, children will take a class walk to seek out and identify patterns around the school and play space. It is helpful to walk the path before taking the children along, so you can identify places to pause and draw the children's attention to particular environmental features during the walk.

Creativity Skills:

Collaboration

Communication

Exploration

Visualization

Activity Steps:

1. Explain to the children that the class will take a walk and look for patterns. Help them understand that patterns can be found everywhere.

2. Drawing their attention to a pattern in the classroom—a window, a wall space, or the floor—can help them start thinking about the possibilities of patterns they might find.

3. Anytime a child points out a pattern during the class walk, pause to draw the children's attention to the pattern. Ask the child who discovered the pattern to explain it to the class.

4. Take digital photographs of the discovered patterns.

Documentation:

Take anecdotal notes on the children's communication and collaboration, exploration, and identification skills. Review the photographs of the patterns found.

Extension Lesson:

Print out the pattern photographs taken on the walk. Ask the children to work together to create a classroom display of the patterns they have discovered. You can help them add descriptive text to accompany the images.

Movement Patterns

Topic: Identify and explore simple patterns through movement

Objective:

Children will participate in collaborative movement patterns.

Creativity Skills:

Collaboration

Communication

Exploration

Materials:

None

Overview:

In this whole-group lesson, the children will participate in a group-movement activity focused on developing simple patterns.

Activity Steps:

1. Ask the children to tell you what they know about patterning. What do they remember from the previous patterning lessons?

2. Talk to the class about making patterns with movements. Demonstrate a simple AB pattern: clap, jump, clap, jump. Invite the

class to stand up and create patterns. Call out the movements and pause occasionally to ask the children what comes next.

3. You can increase the complexity of the game by introducing ABC patterns: clap, stomp, jump, clap, stomp, jump.

4. As the children gain experience, invite them to take turns calling out the movements.

Documentation:

Take anecdotal notes on the children's communication, collaboration, and pattern exploration skills.

Extension Lesson:

You can invite children to make sound patterns with simple musical instruments, such as bells, shakers, and drums.

Pattern Strings

Topic: Identify and create simple patterns

Objective:

Children will identify and create a simple pattern—AB or ABC—by stringing beads.

Materials:

Long pieces of string

Collection of large beads in various colors and shapes

Individual trays

Creativity Skills:

Exploration

Strategic planning

Visualization

Overview:

This activity allows children to create their own patterns by stringing beads. They can easily take beads off and make corrections if they get off track with their patterns.

Please note that small beads can be choking hazards, especially for children under three years old. Choose materials appropriate to the age of the children. Talk with the children about the proper use of the materials, and use caution.

Activity Steps:

1. In advance, cut a 12" piece of string for each child, and tie a knot in one end of each piece. Place individual trays with a piece of string and a collection of beads on a table where children can access them.

2. Introduce the children to the idea of creating patterns with beads by working alongside them. Ask the children to think about patterns they would like to create with the beads. Help them understand how the patterns will repeat.

3. Children will seek out and sort desired beads as necessary. Encourage each child to repeat his core pattern until his string is full.

4. As children finish, ask them to talk about their patterns with others at the table. Specifically, ask the children about the relationships between beads: Which shape of bead comes after the rectangular bead? How did you know that?

5. Pattern strings can be added to a documentation panel or bulletin board to show the children's patterning work.

Documentation:

Take anecdotal notes on children's abilities to recognize and apply attribute information to create simple patterns. You can post the completed string patterns for reference and ideas.

Extension Lesson:

Children can deconstruct their pattern strings and have repeated experiences with creating bead patterns on string. Children can also create beads out of air-dry modeling clay or playdough. Children can paint their dried beads and create personalized pattern strings.

Children's Books

Cleary, Brian P. 2012. *A-B-A-B-A—A Book of Pattern Play*. Minneapolis, MN: Millbrook.
The illustrations help readers explore many examples of repeating sequences of shapes, colors, and objects.

Harris, Trudy. 2000. *Pattern Fish*. Minneapolis, MN: Millbrook.
This book encourages readers to recognize patterns, which are everywhere—in the colors of the fish, the backgrounds, the text, and the borders of each page.

Stockdale, Susan. 1999. *Nature's Paintbrush*. New York: Simon and Schuster.
Through vibrant artwork, this book shows the many colors and patterns to be found in nature.

Index

Note: A *t* following a page number indicates a table.

A

addition. *See* computation; quantification

algebraic thinking, 105

B

Burnard, Pamela, 8

C

cardinality, 22

children's books

    computation, 50

    data collection and statistics, 104

    geometry and spatial sense, 75

    measurement, 91

    numbers and number sense, 35

    patterns and relationships, 116

classroom environments

    developing creative, 13–14

    math learning centers, 14–18

communication, 11*t*

comparison

    lesson ideas for, 40–42, 44–46,
    80–86, 88, 96, 98, 100–101, 103

    and measurement skills, 78

overview of, 76

    See also measurement

computation

    children's books, 50

    lesson ideas for, 40–49

    manipulatives for, 17

    NCTM standards for, 37

    overview of, 36–38

    vocabulary, 36

computational thinking, 38

connections, 11*t*

counting. *See* computation; quantification

counting-on strategy, 36, 47–49

Craft, Anna, 8

creativity, value of, 13

Cremin, Teresa, 8

D

data collection and statistics

    children's books, 104

    graphing, 95–100, 103–104

    lesson ideas for, 96–104

    manipulatives for, 17

    NCTM standards for, 93

overview of, 92

vocabulary, 96

G

geometry and spatial sense, 51

children's books, 75

lesson ideas for, 61–75

manipulatives for, 17

mapping, 60, 71–75

NCTM standards for, 52–53

overview of, 51

position words, 55–58, 69t, 71–75

and shapes, 53–55

and spatial relationships, 55–57

and symmetry, 58–60

graphing, 95–100, 103–104

guided inquiry. *See* inquiry-based

approach

I

IAE. *See* International Academy of

Education (IAE)

inquiry-based approach

components of, 7–8, 9t

and open-ended activities, 13–14

teacher actions for, 9t

International Academy of Education (IAE), 4

L

learning. *See* inquiry-based approach

lesson ideas

for computation, 40–49

for data collection and statistics,

96–104

for geometry and spatial sense,

61–75

for measurement, 80–91

for numbers and number sense,

25–35

and patterns and relationships,

107–115

"loose parts," 18

See also manipulatives

M

manipulatives

for math learning centers, 17–18

for measurement, 79–80

value of, 51

mapping, 58, 60, 71–75

mathematics, as embedded in all

experiences, 1–2, 4

mathematics teaching

inquiry-based approach to, 7–8

and "possibility thinking" concept, 8

principles of effective, 5–6t

math learning centers

    designing, 14–16

    managing, 16–17

    manipulatives for, 17–18

    and technology, 18

measurement

    children's books, 91

    lesson ideas for, 80–91

    manipulatives for, 17, 79–80

    NCTM standards for, 76–77

    overview of, 76

    processes of, 77–78

    of time, 88–91

music, 106

N

National Council of Teachers of

    Mathematics (NCTM) standards

    for algebra, 105–106

    for computation, 37

    for data analysis and probability, 93

    for data collection and statistics, 93

    for geometry and spatial sense,

    52–53

    for measurement, 76–77

    for number and operations, 20–21,

    37

    for number sense, 20–21

    overview, 10–12t

    for patterns and relationships,

    105–106

Nicholson, Simon, 18

numbers and number sense

    cardinality, 22

    children's books, 35

    lesson ideas for, 25–35

    manipulatives for, 17

    NCTM standards for, 20–21

    one-to-one correspondence, 21–22,

    25–27

    overview of, 19–20

    quantification, 22, 23–24

    subitizing, 23

O

one-to-one correspondence

    defined, 21–22

    lesson ideas for, 25–27

open-ended activities, value of, 13–14

P

patterns and relationships

    and algebraic thinking, 105

    children's books, 116

    lesson ideas for, 107–115

    manipulatives for, 17

    NCTM standards for, 105–106

    overview of, 105

play, value of, in learning, 3–4

position words, 1, 55–58, 69t, 71–75

positive mathematics identities, 4

"possibility thinking" concept, 8

problem solving, 10t

Q

quantification

    counting level of, 22

    defined, 23

    global level of, 22

R

reasoning and proof, 11t

relationships. See patterns and

    relationships

representation, 12t

S

shapes, 53–55, 61–71

    See also geometry and spatial sense

small-group work, 14

spatial orientation, 55

spatial relationships, 55–57

spatial sense. See geometry and spatial

    sense

spatial visualization, 55

statistics. See data collection and statistics

storytelling, 46–47

students, interplay of, with teachers, 8

subitizing, 23

subtraction. See computation

symmetry, 58–60

T

teachers

    actions of, for inquiry-based learning,
    9t

    interplay of, with students, 8

teaching. See mathematics teaching

technology, 18

time, 88–91

V

vocabulary

    of computation, 36

    for data collection and statistics, 96

    position words, 55–58, 69t, 71–75

    of time, 88

voting, 92, 94–96, 102–104